THE MITCHELL BEAZLEY POCKET GUIDE TO

Butterflies

Paul Whalley &
Richard Lewington

Abbreviations

For abbreviated place names, see explanation under Names (p 4).

D	distribution		(number of	sp(p)	species
esp	especially		broods in a		(plural)
f.	form		year)	subsp	subspecies
FP	Foodplant	hwing	hindwing	var.	variety
	(of	incl	including	WS	wingspan*
	caterpillar)	m	metre	♂	male
fwing	forewing	mm	millimetre	♀	female
Gen	generation	mts	mountains	cp	compare

* Wingspans given in the text are based on twice the length of one forewing, measured along the costa (front margin) from the base to the apex, plus the width across the body.

Symbols

🌲	Coniferous woods	〰️	Coasts and estuaries
🌳	Broadleaved woods	🌾	Agricultural land and hedgerows
❀	Meadows without trees (wet or dry)	▦	Chalk and limestone areas
🏛	Parkland, meadows with trees	◤	Heathland
〰	Marshland, including rivers and lakes	◣	Moorland
⛰	Mountains	🗺	Occurs in British Isles (as resident or migrant)
◥	Hills and slopes	P	Protected by law in some countries

The Mitchell Beazley Pocket Guide to Butterflies

First published in 1981 by Mitchell Beazley, an imprint of Octopus Publishing Group Ltd, 2–4 Heron Quays, London E14 4JP

© Mitchell Beazley 1981
Illustrations Richard Lewington/The Garden Studio © Mitchell Beazley 1981

Reprinted 1982, 1983, 1984, 1987, 1988, 1990, 1991, 1992
Revised edition 1996, Reprinted 1999, 2003 (twice)

ISBN 1 84000 272 7

Printed and bound by Toppan Printing Company, China

Contents

Introduction

There are about 16,000 species of butterflies in the world, of which about 400 occur in Europe – this guide covers Europe, including the Mediterranean islands. Since the Pocket Guide to Butterflies was first published in 1981 our knowledge of butterflies has increased: new species have been recognized in Europe and further studies of some existing species have shown they are a complex of two or more very similar species. The discovery of these previously unrecognized species of similar butterflies makes identification of these groups difficult.

Fortunately the more common European butterflies are easily recognized in the field. However, in spite of many years of study there is still disagreement both on the actual numbers of species and their relationship. This problem is acute in some genera, e.g. *Hipparchia*, *Oeneis* and *Erebia*, where the similarity between the species makes it difficult to identify them in the field. Sometimes a species formerly considered widespread in Europe has been found to consist of several geographically isolated, but very similar, species. In these cases the locality in which the butterfly is seen will enable the correct identification to be made. Attention is called to these problems either by listing the species or by indicating that the common name may refer to several species, e.g. Green-veined Whites.

The amount of wing pattern exposed when the butterfly is at rest can be an important guide to its identification. The illustrations show the wings spread out to reveal all the pattern; this may not always be visible at rest. With the exception of the Monarch, all are illustrated approximately life-size.

Scientific names

There is currently little agreement on the combination of scientific names that should be used for European Lepidoptera. With this in mind it was decided that, in spite of the need to change some scientific names in this field-guide, they would follow the check-list published in Volume 8 of a partially completed multi-volume work on European Lepidoptera edited by O. Kudrna.

Scientific names used in earlier editions of this field-guide will be found in the Index, enabling easy reference to any changes. Many of the changes here revert to earlier usage where the generic names emphasize the similarities between included species rather than their (often small) differences.

These changes have no effect on the use of the guide for identification and are cross-referenced in the Index.

Names

The Camberwell Beauty butterfly is also known as the Willow Beauty or White Petticoat; on the Continent it is called Le Morio, Antiopa, Trauermantel, Sorgmantel, etc. Scientific names of animals and plants, however, are an international language enabling communication across frontiers. Whatever the popular name of the butterfly more usually known (in Britain) as the Camberwell Beauty, its scientific name, *Nymphalis antiopa*, will be understood in any language.

The scientific name of a butterfly consists of at least two words. The first word, the generic name, is always written with a capital letter and includes groups of related, and often fairly similar, species. The second word, often loosely referred to as the specific name, starts with a lower-case letter. When used with a generic name it forms a unique combination.

For example, *Papilio machaon*, the Swallowtail, is related to the Corsican Swallowtail, *Papilio hospiton*, as shown by their generic names, *Papilio*. The unique combination of generic and specific name, *Papilio machaon*, can only refer to one species, the Swallowtail. The Scarce Swallowtail, *Iphiclides podalirius*, is less closely related and belongs to a different genus, *Iphiclides*.

While the second scientific (specific) names are now generally accepted for most European Lepidoptera, the generic names, indicating the relationships between species, are more liable to be altered according to the latest ideas.

Sometimes local populations of a widespread species differ slightly and may be named as subspecies. This is indicated by the third, or subspecific, scientific name, e.g. *hibernica* in the combination *Euphydryas aurinia hibernica*. Individual variation within a species or subspecies may also be given an additional form or aberration name.

Czech Czech Republic and Slovakia
Scand Scandinavia, includes Denmark, Norway, Sweden and Finland
Scot Scotland
Switz Switzerland
Yug Former Yugoslavia

[*D:*]:- the distribution in Europe is given in broad terms, partly from limited space but also because of lack of precise data. The book includes more species found from the Arctic circle to the Mediterranean, including the main islands, but not North Africa. Mention of a particular country only indicates that a species should be found in suitable habitats in that country and may not be widespread. Where Britain is specifically excluded from the range, it can be assumed that the species does not occur in Ireland.

[*Flight:*]:- the earliest and last months in which the butterfly may be seen. This varies according to weather but is even more dependent on latitude in Europe.

[*FP:*]:- a broad guide to the foodplant of the caterpillar of the species. Lack of space restricts us to including the most frequently chosen food only. 'Grasses' indicates that the caterpillar may feed on one (or more) species of grass. In most cases the particular preferences are now known.

[*Gen:*]:- the number of generations completed each year (i.e. from egg to adult). This may vary within one species according to temperature and latitude in Europe. There are usually more generations each year in southerly latitudes of a species whose range extends from north to south Europe.

[*WS:*]:- the distance between the tips of the out-stretched forewings. This measurement takes into account some of the variation in wingspan within species. Few butterflies actually sit with the wings fully expanded in the field and this must be taken into account when estimating wingspan.

References

A Field Guide to the Butterflies of Britain and Europe L. G. Higgins and N. D. Riley, Collins, London, 1980

British Butterflies, A Field Guide Robert Goodden, David and Charles, Newton Abbot, 1978

The Classification of European Butterflies L. G. Higgins, Collins, London, 1975

South's British Butterflies T. G. Howarth, Warne, London, 1973

Butterflies in Colour L. Lyneborg, Blandford Press, London, 1974

Butterfly Watching Paul Whalley, Severn House, London, 1980

Hamlyn Nature Guide, Butterflies Paul Whalley, Hamlyn, London, 1979

The Observer's Book of Caterpillars David J. Carter, Warne, London, 1979

Wild Flowers of Britain and Northern Europe R. G. Fitter, A. Fitter and M. Blamey, Collins, London, 1974

The Concise Flowers of Europe Oleg Polunin, Warne, London, 1979

The Butterflies of Britain and Europe L. G. Higgins, Collins, London, 1983

The Butterflies of Britain and Ireland J. Thomas and R. Lewington, Dorling Kindersley, London, 1991

The Butterflies of Scandinavia in Nature H. J. Henrikson and I. B. Kreutzer, Skandinavisk Bogforlag, Odense, 1982

Butterflies of Europe O. Kudrna, Vol. 8, Aula-Verlag, Wiesbaden, 1986

The Moths and Butterflies of Gt Britain and Ireland Vol. 7(1), A. M. Emmet and John Heath, Harley Books, Colchester, Essex, 1989

Ecology and Conservation of Butterflies [edited] A. S. Pullin, Chapman & Hall, London, 1995

Butterfly Watching, P. Whalley, Hamlyn Paperback, London, 1983

The Butterfly Gardener M. Rothschild and C. Farrell, Michael Joseph/Rainbird, London, 1983

The structure of a butterfly

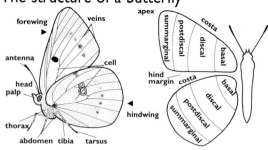

Butterflies are covered by scales which easily rub off if they are handled. Each individual scale forms a small part of the colour and pattern. They are important for butterfly survival and may be used in different ways. Colour and pattern are also used in field-guides for identification.

Some colours, such as red, warn predators that the butterfly is distasteful or poisonous. The round 'peacock-eye' pattern on the wings of many butterflies is flashed at birds or small mammals to mimic the eyes of a larger animal. Butterflies at rest show the undersides if their wings which are generally a duller colour than the uppersides. In this way they blend well into their surroundings.

The colours themselves may be produced by pigments within each scale, for example white or red, or by the actual shape of the surface of the scale which reflects the light in different ways. This gives the iridescent or metallic colours, often purple or blue. Mixtures of scales and patches of them produce the patterns on the wings which give butterflies the glorious colours that we see.

Their compound eyes, which are made up of many separate parts (facets), are sensitive to wave-lengths of light far beyond human vision.

Females need to recognize the plant on which their caterpillars will feed. Although a few species whose caterpillars feed on a wide range of plants do not have to be selective and scatter their eggs in the grass, most female butterflies carefully select a plant for egg-laying. To find suitable plants they must be sensitive not only to the flower colour but also to the scent of the plant. They have an ability to detect scents at very low concentrations and to fly towards their source. There are numerous sense organs which may be used to detect scents, many of which are situated on their antennae. There are also specialized receptors in the tips of their legs through which they can 'taste' the plant on which they are settled. Chemical scents (pheromones) are produced by both sexes and are important in attracting one another.

Although many insects have a proboscis (the feeding tube below the head), only in butterflies and moths is it a coiled tube that, when fully extended, enables them to suck up liquid. This very long proboscis is able to reach deep into a flower for the hidden nectar. The proboscis of a tropical hawk-moth when extended is 30 cm. It reaches the nectar deep inside an orchid. To fly from plant to plant without being able to curl this up under the head would be impossible.

Life history

Although the life span of some adult butterflies may be only a few days, their whole life cycle is longer. It includes the egg, caterpillar and chrysalis and this may last from a few weeks to several years. With smaller butterflies, particularly in warmer weather, the adult may live for a week whereas larger butterflies, especially those that hibernate during the northern winter, may live for 10 or more months.

The female butterfly generally lays large numbers of eggs; some of these will probably be eaten or parasitized. From the surviving eggs the caterpillars hatch, moult and grow. If they avoid being eaten by hungry birds or mammals, they form their chrysalis in which metamorphosis, the change into a butterfly, takes place. The chrysalides are sought as food by many animals so it is not surprising that very few adult butterflies are eventually produced from a large number of eggs.

Butterfly watching

Like bird watching, this requires patience but, unlike bird watching, which can take place in freezing weather, butterfly watching is best on warm, sunny days.

The apparently aimless flight of a butterfly conceals its more positive activity. Recent research has shown that many butterflies, particularly the males, patrol along well-defined territories such as flowery banks. They will chase out any other intruding male but encourage the females to stay.

Their attraction to flowers is well-known; what is not fully understood is why some colours are more attractive to them and whether the attraction is more evident at different times of day. Watching butterflies on flowers will provide some information about their behaviour; these, and other observations on their daily life, are needed before we can begin fully to understand their behaviour. While it is possible to use binoculars to watch butterflies, the ideal instrument is the short-focus telescope. This instrument, 80–90 mm long, has revolutionized their study, enabling us to magnify the butterfly and study it more closely than is otherwise possible.

Photography is the best way of 'collecting' butterflies. Modern cameras are so well-equipped that it is relatively easy to get pictures even with a standard lens. As you get more involved you will find that you need a close-up (macro) lens. With an automatic-focus camera and all the other facilities available it is less difficult to get an attractive picture.

Getting to know butterflies in your local area will lead to an understanding of their behaviour and distribution. You can quickly become an expert on your favourite spot simply by being aware of the species occurring there, when to see them and the changes throughout the year.

If you start counting the numbers of one or more of the species you see on a regular walk you will begin to build up a picture of the fluctuations in numbers. A standard method of counting uses an imaginary 5 m box around the walker. All the butterflies within this distance on either side and in front are counted. The walk can be divided up according to the type

Mating position of the Common blue (*Polyommatus icarus*)

of vegetation in that stretch and the figures for the total numbers of butterflies in each section counted. The same walk should ideally be carried out once a week in broadly similar weather from April to September. Details of the weather, vegetation and a map of the walk will all form part of the records that will give an estimate of the fluctuations of the butterflies locally. This technique has been used over a number of years by different observers and gives comparable results.

Butterflies can be encouraged into your garden by planting flowers that provide nectar and scent. Plants like buddleia, Michaelmas daisy, ice plant, lavender and many others will attract butterflies (see References). Questions to be asked include: To which flowers are butterflies attracted? Do they spend longer feeding on one flower than another? Do they often feed on flowers in the sun? These and many other topics can be studied in your garden.

Most countries now have their own societies for the study of butterflies. Two which have a broad interest in Europe are:

Societas Europaea Lepidopterologica, c/o Landessammlungen fur Naturkunde, Erbprinzenstrasse 13, D-75000, Karlsruhe 1, Germany.

The Butterfly Conservation Society, P.O. Box 222, Dedham, Colchester, Essex CO7 6EY, UK.

Conservation

Charles Darwin's evolutionary writings gave rise to the phrase 'survival of the fittest'. Nature conservation over recent years can perhaps be characterized by 'survival of the less fit'. The emphasis has been on conserving rare or endangered species that are struggling to survive. While this has helped the survival of some species, the concentration of resources has meant that the more common species have had very little attention.

Although we talk about conservation of species, we should really call it habitat conservation. It is little use providing laws to protect a species if its habitat can be freely destroyed. All habitats tend to change naturally with time, whether a grassland is gradually covered with scrub and, eventually, with trees, or a pond fills up with encroaching reeds and then dries out. It is clear that, as these vegetational changes take place, the fauna will also change as the area becomes less suitable for the existing species and more suitable for others. One aim of conservation is to slow down this natural succession by various forms of habitat management. This can involve intervention in the area in quite dramatic ways to conserve the existing fauna.

Intervention may involve clearing shrubs to maintain an area of grass; it may even mean removing or coppicing trees to reduce shady areas. All intervention which may help one or more species will inevitably have some harmful effect on other species, so it is important that the negative effects of any intervention are considered. For example, clearing hawthorn to maintain areas for grass-loving species may be a good idea for those species, but will not help the hawthorn shield-bug or other animals dependent on hawthorn.

Grasslands that are well-grazed will have short turf favouring certain species. If there is less grazing, perhaps if the sheep are removed or the rabbits die out, then the grass will grow longer and the butterfly fauna will change. Other factors, like shallow soil or continuous sea-spray exposure, may help to keep the grass short.

Maintaining the biodiversity of the habitat is currently a popular objective. This aims to maintain as many species as possible in the habitat. A diverse habitat should provide many suitable places (niches) for a number of different species. Within this diverse area, each individual niche may be quite small and this can mean that species dependent on each niche are present only in small numbers. Any damage to the habitat would be likely to destroy several specialized niches, and this could lead to extinction of the species dependent on them. The fragility of parts of diverse habitats is possibly one of the weaknesses. Perhaps this is why the use of biodiversity as a measure of conservation success is now being challenged.

The counter argument is that, in a more uniform habitat with fewer species, there would be larger numbers of each individual species. This is a better conservation practice, it is argued, because numbers are high so any one species is in less danger of extinction if part of the habitat is damaged.

Conservation is choice; we have to select the species or habitats we would like to protect. Most of us have a different idea of what species we want to conserve, and we measure success by the survival of our 'favourite' species or habitat.

Skippers Hesperiidae

There are about 40 species of skippers in Europe, eight of which occur in Britain. They have a rapid whirring or skipping flight, and short, broad bodies and even broader heads bearing two widely separated pointed antennae. At rest they hold their wings like those of a moth – either spread out flat or with the fore- and hindwings at separate angles to each other.

Large grizzled skipper

Pyrgus alveus

Underside hindwing olive-brown to green with white marks

Hindwing has faint white spots

A variable-patterned butterfly with many subspecies. It is often confused with the Safflower skipper (p 13), but may be distinguished by the more widely spaced white spots in the cell of the forewing. Widespread and found on flowery slopes between 900 and 1800 m. *WS:* 22–32 mm; *Flight:* June–Aug; *Gen:* 1–2; *FP:* Cinquefoil (*Potentilla*), Rock rose (*Helianthemum*), Blackberry (*Rubus*); *D:* Europe (not Britain, Denmark, Holland, N Scand). *P. warrenensis* (Warren's skipper) is similar but smaller with tiny white markings. *WS:* 18–24 mm; *D:* Alps (France, Switz).

Grizzled skipper

P. malvae

White markings well-defined on both wings; margins alternately marked light and dark

Hindwing has clear row of small postdiscal spots

Underside green-brown varying to yellowish

In Britain the Grizzled skipper is chiefly confined to central and southern England, with a few colonies in Wales. It flies rapidly and close to the ground over bogs and flowery meadows up to 2000 m, pausing to rest on bare soils with its wings held erect over its back. A 2nd generation usually occurs in warmer parts of southern Europe, but rarely further north. The Grizzled skipper is one of the few British species to overwinter as a pupa. *WS:* 22–26 mm; *Flight:* Apr–June, July–Aug; *Gen:* 2; *FP:* Wild strawberry (*Fragaria vesca*), Cinquefoil (*Potentilla*), Mallow (*Malva*); *D:* C, N and E Europe.

Southern grizzled skipper

P. malvoides

Externally identical to *P. malvae*, some consider it a subspecies. (Structure of genitalia differs.) *WS:* 22–32 mm; *Flight:* Apr–Aug; *Gen:* 2; *FP:* as *P. malvae*; *D:* S France, Spain, Portugal, Italy, S. Switz, Sicily.

Oberthur's grizzled skipper

P. armoricanus

Uppers resemble
P. alveus; darker when
first emerged

Hindwing
markings pale
but distinct

**Underside
hindwing** has
large central
spot

♂

Widespread throughout Europe but more common in the south, Oberthur's grizzled skipper feeds on flowers of dry, hilly scrubland up to 1200 m. The 2nd generation, found only in southern parts, has a smaller wingspan. *WS:* 24–28 mm; *Flight:* May–June, Aug–Sept; *Gen:* 2; *FP:* Wild strawberry (*Fragaria vesca*), Cinquefoil (*Potentilla*); *D:* Europe (not Britain, Holland, most of Scand except for few records in Denmark and S Sweden).

Foulquier's grizzled skipper

P. foulquieri

♂

Underside hindwing
more white on wing than
in *P. alveus*

Hindwing pale marks
form band across wing

♂

The female often has a pale yellow suffusion over the upperside and smaller white markings. As with other grizzled skippers, Foulquier's grizzled skipper is extremely difficult to identify in the field, and a close examination is nearly always required. It is locally common in southern Europe on mountain slopes up to 2000 m. A smaller, yellower subspecies occurs in Italy. *WS:* 26–30 mm; *Flight:* July–Aug; *Gen:* 1; *FP:* Cinquefoil (*Potentilla*); *D:* S and C France, N Spain, Italy.

Olive skipper

P. serratulae

♂

Forewing spots
generally small

Hindwing
almost
unmarked,
spots indistinct

**Underside
hindwing**
olive-green to
grey-green

♂

The Olive skipper is locally common in mountainous districts up to 2500 m, especially in southeastern Europe. It has a rapid flight and settles on bare patches of ground. A larger species, *P. serratulae major*, has a darker underside and clearer white markings. *WS:* 24–28 mm; *Flight:* July–Aug; *Gen:* 1; *FP:* Cinquefoil (*Potentilla*); *D:* S and C Europe (not Britain, NW France, Holland, Scand).

Carline skipper

Pyrgus carlinae ♂

Forewing white mark in cell curved outwards like a 'C'

Hindwing marks pale and obscure

Underside hwing pale red-brown with large white mark near margin

In the wetter areas of the southwestern Alps, up to 2500 m, the Carline skipper may often be seen assembling in large numbers. It has the typical rapid flight of skippers, and when at rest the reddish tinge to the underside hindwing distinguishes it from the Olive skipper (p. 11). It has smaller, less distinct markings on its upperside than the Cinquefoil skipper. *WS:* 26–28 mm; *Flight:* late June–Aug; *Gen:* 1; *FP:* Spring cinquefoil (*Potentilla verna*); *D:* Alps (S France, Austria, Switz, Italy).

Cinquefoil skipper

P. cirsii

Fwing has squarish white spot in cell

Underside hwing olive-yellow to reddish-brown

A local species with a quick, darting flight, the Cinquefoil skipper may be found in flowery meadows up to 1500 m. Some authorities list this skipper as a subspecies of the Carline skipper, for it is known that they breed together where their territories overlap. *WS:* 26–28 mm; *Flight:* July–Aug; *Gen:* 1; *FP:* Spring cinquefoil (*Potentilla verna*); *D:* Spain, Portugal, C France (inc Pyrenees), Germany, Switz, Austria, Corsica.

Rosy grizzled skipper

P. onopordi ♂

Pale yellow suffusion over dark brown ground colour. Pattern on forewing well-defined

Underside hindwing has anvil-shaped mark near centre

The Rosy grizzled skipper has a preference for the same kind of habitat as the Cinquefoil skipper and may be distinguished by the generally larger white patches on the underside hindwing and the paler, yellower upperside. The female is often slightly larger than the male and has fewer yellow scales. *WS:* 22–28 mm; *Flight:* Apr–June, July–Sept; *Gen:* 2; *FP:* Cinquefoil (*Potentilla*); *D:* Spain, Portugal, S France, Italy (records from the Mediterranean islands need confirmation).

Yellow-banded skipper

P. sidae

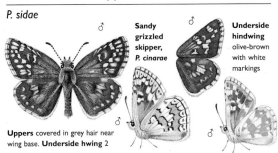

♂ **Sandy grizzled skipper, P. cinarae** ♂ **Underside hindwing** olive-brown with white markings

Uppers covered in grey hair near wing base. **Underside hwing 2**

This species flies over flowery meadows up to 1500 m. There is a smaller Italian subspecies with paler bands underneath. *WS:* 32–38 mm; *Flight:* June–July; *Gen:* 1; *FP: Abutilon avicennae*; *D:* S France, Italy, Greece, Yug, Bulgaria, Romania.

Sandy grizzled skipper, *P. cinarae*, prefers dry stony hills up to 1000 m. Female has smaller spots on uppers. *WS:* 30–32 mm; *Flight:* June; *FP:* unknown; *D:* Yug, Albania, Bulgaria, C Spain.

Safflower skipper

P. carthami

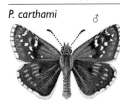 ♂

♀ is larger and less hairy

Hindwing has regular row of postdiscal spots

Underside hindwing strongly mottled, white markings edged in grey

 ♂

The Safflower skipper is a widely distributed and often locally common butterfly of meadows and hillsides up to 1500 m. The Spanish form has larger white markings. *WS:* 30–34 mm; *Flight:* June–Sept; *Gen:* 1; *FP:* Hollyhock (*Althaea*), Mallow (*Malva*); *D:* S and C Europe (not N France, Britain, Holland, Scand).

Alpine grizzled skipper

P. andromedae

 ♂

Pattern well-defined on forewing, but not on hindwing

Underside hwing has white streak and round spot near lower edge

 ♂

Preferring the damp habitat offered by mountain lakes, the Alpine grizzled skipper may be found flying up to 1500 m in the Pyrenees and Alps, although further north in Scandinavia it is considered to be a lowland species. It commonly occurs within the Arctic Circle. *WS:* 26–30 mm; *Flight:* June–July; *Gen:* 1; *FP:* unknown; *D:* N Scand, France (Pyrenees, Alps), N Spain, Austria, Switz, Yug, Bulgaria.

Dusky grizzled skipper

Pyrgus cacaliae

♂

Spots on upper forewing
very small, absent on
hindwing

Markings on underside
not as sharp as in
P. andromedae

♂

Similar to the Alpine grizzled skipper (p 13) but with less white
on its forewings, the Dusky grizzled skipper has a rapid, whirring
flight and lives in mountainous regions above 2000 m. *WS*: 26–30
mm; *Flight:* June–Aug; *Gen:* 1; *FP:* Coltsfoot (*Tussilago farfara*);
D: Austria, Switz, France (Alps), Pyrenees, Romania, Bulgaria.

Northern grizzled skipper

P. centaureae

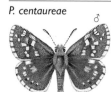

♂

Both wings are dark
brown with prominent
white spots

Veins lined white on
the underside are
characteristic

♂

This rather grey-brown species may be seen rapidly flying over
bogs, moorlands and tundra up to 1000 m. It is locally common
throughout the mountainous regions of Scandinavia, but is noticeably absent from the cultivated southern part. *WS*: 26–30 mm;
Flight: June–July; *Gen:* 1; *FP:* Cloudberry (*Rubus chamaemorus*);
D: Scand.

Red underwing skipper

Spialia sertorius

♂

White spots
small, pattern
variable on
uppers

**Persian
skipper,
S. phlomidis,**
has larger
white spots
on uppers

♂

Distinguished by dark
red or red-brown
underside hindwing

Olive-grey
underside
hindwing

This small skipper with many subspecies, is locally common on
mountains up to 1400 m. The second generation is smaller. *WS*:
22–26 mm; *Flight:* Apr–Aug; *Gen:* 2; *FP:* Great burnet (*Sanguisorba*), Raspberry (*Rubus*), Cinquefoil (*Potentilla*); *D:* Spain, Portugal, France, Italy, S Germany, Switz, Austria, Yug.
Persian skipper, S. phlomidis at lower altitudes. *WS*: 28–30 mm;
Flight: June–July; *FP:* unknown; *D:* Greece, Albania, SE Yug.

Hungarian skipper

S. orbifer ♂

Forewing has regular row of submarginal spots

Underside hindwing has round costal spot

Once thought a subspecies of *S. sertorius* (p 14), this species is separated by its olive-green underside hindwing. Flies over rough ground up to 1600 m. *WS:* 22–28 mm; *Flight:* Apr–Aug; *Gen:* 2; *FP* Cinquefoil (*Potentilla*), Burnet (*Sanguisorba*); *D:* E. Europe.

Tessellated skipper

Cycagnicus tessellum

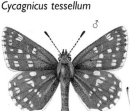

Spinose skipper, C. cribrellum

Markings clearer, longer

Uppers well marked. **Underside** more olive-brown than *C. cribrellum*

C. tessellum is not a well-known skipper, occurs in flowery grassland up to 1000 m. *WS:* 32–36 mm; *Flight:* May–June; *Gen:* 1; *FP: Phlomis tuberosa*; *D:* Greece, SE Yug.
Spinose skipper, C. cribrellum is also little-known. Found in dry, treeless countryside, it may be distinguished by the clear white marks, especially near the wing margin, the yellowish underside hindwing and its smaller size. *WS:* 26–32 mm; *Flight:* late May–June; *Gen:* 1; *FP:* Cinquefoil (*Potentilla*); *D:* Romania.

Sage skipper

C. proto ♂

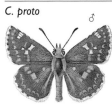

Forewing has white, well-marked central spot

Underside yellow-grey to reddish with pale markings

Submarginal spots obscure on both wings

A rapid flyer, prone to variation in wing pattern, the Sage skipper is locally common on lowland grassland and mountain slopes up to 1700 m. The female is similar but has less hair near the wing base. In late summer the species is often smaller with a more reddish-brown underside hindwing. *WS:* 28–30 mm; *Flight:* Apr–Sept; *Gen:* 1; *FP:* Jerusalem sage (*Phlomis fruticosa*); *D:* S France, Spain, Portugal, Italy, Sicily, Greece, Yug.

Mallow skipper

Carcharodus alceae

♂

Uppers brown with darker marbling

♂

Hindwing markings indistinct

Underside fwing ♂ lacks tuft

The first generation is darker than the second. Flies over flowery slopes up to 1500 m. *WS:* 26–34 mm; *Flight:* Apr–Aug; *Gen:* 2 (1 at high altitudes); *FP:* Mallow (*Malva*), Hollyhock (*Althaea*); *D:* S and C Europe (not Britain, Holland, N Germany, Scand).

Marbled skipper

C. lavatherae

♂

Fwing olive-green with darker marbling and white spots

Hwing darker with large central spots and arrow-shaped postdiscal spots

Fwing not tufted; **hwing** pale green

♂

Local on dry chalky slopes up to 1800 m. *WS:* 28–34 mm; *Flight:* May–Aug; *Gen:* 1, possibly 2; *FP:* Woundwort (*Stachys*); *D:* S and C Europe (not Corsica, Sardinia, Sicily), rare north of the Alps.

Tufted marbled skipper

C. flocciferus

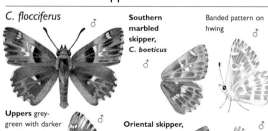

♂

Southern marbled skipper, C. boeticus

♂

Banded pattern on hwing

♂

Uppers grey-green with darker marbling and large spots on forewing
Underside fwing has hair tuft

♂

Oriental skipper, C. orientalis, underside hwing marks regular, fwing tufted

♂

WS: 28–32 mm; *Flight:* May–Sept; *Gen:* 2–3; *FP:* White horehound (*Marrubium vulgare*); *D:* S and C Europe.
Southern marbled skipper, *C. boeticus*. *WS:* 26–28 mm; *Flight:* May–Oct; *Gen:* 2–3; *FP:* as for *C. flocciferus*; *D:* Spain, Portugal, S France, Italy, Switz.
Oriental skipper, *C. orientalis*. *WS:* 28–30 mm; *Flight:* Apr–Sept; *Gen:* 2–3; *FP:* unknown; *D:* Albania, Greece, Yug, Bulgaria.

Large chequered skipper

Heteropterus morpheus

♂

Uppers dark brown, unmarked, but for pale yellow patches near front edge of forewing

Underside hwing has large, ringed spots

♂

Scattered colonies occur throughout Europe in damp meadows. Recognized by its underside pattern. *WS:* 32–38 mm; *Flight:* June–Aug; *Gen:* 1; *FP:* grasses (*Juncus*), esp Brome (*Bromus*); *D:* N Spain, France, Germany, Holland, S Scand, Italy, Switz, E Europe.

Dingy skipper

Erynnis tages

♂

Inky skipper, *E. marloyi*, has dark brown uppers and unders, unmarked for spot on forewing

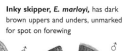 

♂

Uppers dark grey-brown, with complete row of white marginal dots on forewing. **Underside** paler, sparsely marked

E. tages is widespread in a variety of open habitats up to 1800 m. *WS:* 26–38 mm; *Flight:* May–June; *Gen:* 1 (2 in south); *FP:* Birds-foot trefoil (*Lotus corniculatus*); *D:* Europe (not N Scand).
Inky skipper, *E. marloyi*, is a mountain species. *WS:* 28–30 mm; *Flight:* May–June; *Gen:* 1; *FP:* unknown; *D:* Greece, Albania, S Yug.

Chequered skipper

Carterocephalus palaemon

♀

Patches on wings may vary in size

♂

♀

Uppers dark brown, chequered with deep yellow patches

♂ ♀ slightly larger, usually with less distinct markings

Underside wing brown, tinged yellow, with pale yellow spots

Underside similar to ♂, but more heavily dusted with yellow scales

This species is now thought to be extinct in England, surviving only very locally in Scotland. It is found in open woodland. *WS:* 28–29 mm; *Flight:* June–July; *Gen:* 1; *FP:* grasses, esp Brome (*Bromus*); *D:* Europe (not Spain, Portugal, Italy, Ireland, Holland).

Northern chequered skipper

Carterocephalus silvicolus

Forewing yellow with brown spots

Hindwing similar to *C. palaemon*, but has extra spot near costa

♀ has more extensive dark areas

♂

Even heavily marked examples of this species are never as dark as the Chequered skipper (p 17). Locally common in wooded valleys. *WS:* 24-26 mm; *Flight:* June-July; *Gen:* 1; *FP:* grasses, esp Dog's-tail (*Cynosurus*); *D:* N Germany, Poland, Scand.

Lulworth skipper

Thymelicus acteon

♂

Uppers golden brown. **Forewing** pale marks in semi-circle; sex brand (dark line) prominent

♂ **Underside** relatively unmarked

♀

Uppers darker brown. **Forewing** yellow spots more conspicuous; sex brand absent

♀ **Palps** white in both sexes

The Lulworth skipper is locally common at altitudes of up to 1600 m in the south, but is rarer further north. In Britain it is restricted to the coast of Devon and Dorset. There are several sub-species which vary in size and colour. *WS:* 22–26 mm; *Flight:* May–Aug; *Gen:* 1; *FP:* grasses, esp Brome (*Bromus*); *D:* Europe (not Scand, Ireland, Holland, Corsica, Sardinia.)

Essex skipper

T. lineola ♂

Uppers tawny brown. **Forewing** (♂ only) as thin black interrupted line (sex brand) parallel to wing edge

♂ Antennal tips black underneath

The key distinguishing feature of both this species and the Small skipper (p 19) is the coloration of the underside of the tips of the antennae. The southeastern counties form the main breeding ground in England, but in the rest of Europe it is widespread in flowery meadows up to 1800 m. *WS:* 24–28 mm; *Flight:* May–Aug; *Gen:* 1; *FP:* grasses; *D:* Europe (not Ireland, N Scand).

Small skipper

T. sylvestris

♂

Uppers tawny brown as in Essex skipper, but sex brand is long, curving

Antennal tips orange underneath

♂

Underside forewing orange-red

The Small skipper is more abundant than the very similar Essex skipper (p 18), its range in Britain covering most of Wales and southern and central England as far north as Yorkshire. It has the typical rapid flight of skippers, often pausing to rest on the ground with its hindwings spread out flat and its forewings raised. It is common in flowery fields and hills up to 1800 m. *WS:* 26–30 mm; *Flight:* June–Aug; *Gen:* 1; *FP:* grasses; *D:* Europe. include Denmark (not rest of Scand, Ireland, Scotl).

Silver-spotted skipper

Hesperia comma

♂

Uppers orange-brown with paler spots
Forewing (♂ only) has prominent ridged sex brand

♂

Underside hindwing olive-green with silver spots

The habitat of the Silver-spotted skipper is mainly the rough grassy fields of chalky and limestone areas up to 2500 m. Numbers have drastically declined in Britain so that only a few scattered colonies remain in southern England. The female lacks a sex brand and is both larger and darker than the male with more extensive spots. *WS:* 28–30 mm; *Flight:* July–Aug; *Gen:* 1; *FP:* grasses; *D:* Europe (not Ireland, S Italy, Corsica, Sardinia).

Large skipper

Ochlodes venatus

♂

Forewing sex brand conspicuous (not in ♀)

Dark veins on orange-brown background

♂

Underside yellowish, faint marks on hindwing

Common species in meadows, chalk downs and woodland edges., May also occur in coastal areas. The plain underside makes it easy to distinguish from the more local Silver-spotted skipper. A very active butterfly, rarely staying long at any one flower. *WS:* 28–34 mm; *Flight:* June–Aug; *Gen:* 1 (2 in south); *FP:* various grasses; *D:* Europe (not Scot, Ireland, N Scand, Corsica, Sardinia).

Mediterranean skipper

Gegenes nostrodamus

♂

Pointed wing tip

Uppers pale brown, without any markings

Underside paler than topside, fading towards wing margin

♂

♀

♀ is larger than ♂ with small spots on both sides of forewing

♀

This skipper has been recorded flying at low altitudes in many locations around the Mediterranean coast, but especially near dry river beds. Has paler, more sandy brown uppersides than the Pigmy skipper. *WS:* 30–32 mm; *Flight:* May–Oct; *Gen:* 2; *FP:* grasses; *D:* Spain, Portugal, Italy, Sicily, Greece, Yug.

Pigmy skipper

G. pumilio

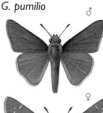

♂

Wing tip slightly pointed

Uppers dark brown, unmarked

Underside uniformly coloured except for a few marks

♂

♀

♀ paler, often larger than ♂, with small spots on forewing, fewer than on the ♀ *G. nostrodamus*

♀

♂

Forewing (both sides) has a row of translucent spots

Zeller's skipper, *Borbo borbonica*

♂

G. pumilio, another Mediterranean coast skipper, often rests on the ground in full sun. *WS:* 26–28 mm; *Flight:* Apr–Oct, *Gen:* 2 or more; *FP:* grasses; *D:* S Spain, S France, Italy, Sicily, Yug, Greece.
Zeller's skipper, *Borbo borbonica* has been reported in various coastal areas of the Mediterranean. *WS:* 28–30 mm; *Flight:* Sept–Oct; *Gen:* 1–2; *FP:* unknown; *D:* Gibraltar.

Swallowtails Papilionidae

Swallowtails are generally large, well-patterned butterflies with slow, flapping flight which can be considerably quickened if pursued. All have three pairs of legs, each of which ends in a single apical claw but, contrary to popular belief, not all species have 'tails' on the posterior margin of the hindwing. There are over 600 species of swallowtails in the world, but only 11 are European, and, of these, *Papilio machaon* is the sole British representative. The caterpillars, by way of a defensive mechanism, have a brightly coloured, eversible gland, or osmeterium, just behind the head, which can be extruded to produce a pungent smell if they are threatened.

Swallowtail caterpillar

Bright colour warns off predators. Foodplant may contain toxins

Swallowtail

Papilio machaon

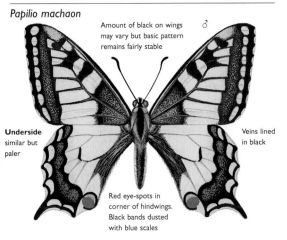

Amount of black on wings may vary but basic pattern remains fairly stable ♂

Underside similar but paler

Veins lined in black

Red eye-spots in corner of hindwings. Black bands dusted with blue scales

The Swallowtail, easily recognized by its striking appearance, is a fast and agile flyer, likely only to be confused with the very local Corsican swallowtail or the Southern swallowtail (p 22). Problems of identification should not occur in Britain, therefore, as this is the only resident swallowtail, with a range restricted to the low-lying fens of East Anglia. The more widely distributed continental subspecies, which flies over flowery meadows to 2000 m, occasionally occurs as a migrant in southern England. Differing slightly in wing pattern, it is a paler yellow than the British Swallowtail, and the black band on the forewing has straighter edges. The first generation is generally darker than the second, although in more northerly areas the appearance of the second brood largely depends on the warmth of the summer. Sex differences are small: the female tends to be larger with less angular wings. *WS:* 64–100 mm; *Flight:* Apr–Aug; *Gen:* 2–3; *FP:* Milk parsley (*Peucedanum palustre*), Wild carrot (*Daucus carota*), Fennel (*Foeniculum vulgare*); *D:* Europe (not Ireland, Scot).

Corsican swallowtail

Papilio hospiton

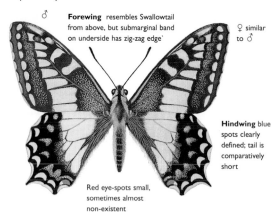

♂

Forewing resembles Swallowtail from above, but submarginal band on underside has zig-zag edge

♀ similar to ♂

Hindwing blue spots clearly defined; tail is comparatively short

Red eye-spots small, sometimes almost non-existent

The Corsican swallowtail, very similar in appearance to the Swallowtail (p 21), may be distinguished by the wavy submarginal band on the underside of its forewing. A local species, it is found only in the mountainous regions of Corsica and Sardinia between 600 and 1500 m. *WS:* 72–76 mm; *Flight:* May–July; *Gen:* probably only 1; *FP:* Giant fennel (*Ferula communis*) and other *Umbelliferae*, *D:* Corsica, Sardinia.

Southern swallowtail

P. alexanor

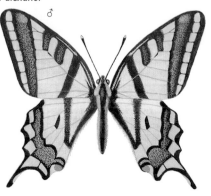

♂

Forewing yellow basal area is diagnostic; submarginal band generally paler than in the related swallowtails

♀ similar but larger

A rare and very local species, the Southern swallowtail is most likely to be seen on the Alpine slopes up to 1300 m. This rapid and powerful flyer is attracted towards thistles, on which it feeds. *WS:* 62–66 mm; *Flight:* Apr–July; *Gen:* 1; *FP: Umbelliferae,* esp Mountain-meadow seseli (*Seseli montanum*), *Trinia vulgaris*, *Ptychotis heterophylla*; *D:* S France (Alps), S Italy, Sicily, Greece, Albania, Yug.

Scarce swallowtail

Iphiclides podalirius

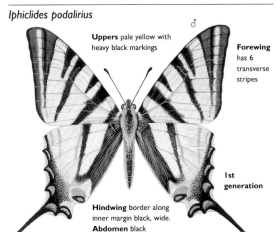

Uppers pale yellow with heavy black markings

Forewing has 6 transverse stripes

♂

1st generation

Hindwing border along inner margin black, wide. **Abdomen** black

Not 'scarce', this has recently become less common. In spring it congregates in hilly areas up to 1600 m but in summer prefers lowland orchards and woods. A 2nd generation, found only in the south, has cream uppers with lighter markings and a white-tipped abdomen. *WS:* 64–80 mm; *Flight:* Mar–Sept; *Gen:* 1 or 2; *FP:* Sloe, Cherry, Hawthorn, and other cultivated fruit trees; *D:* Europe (not Britain, N Scand, Spain; migrant to Holland, Denmark, S Sweden).

Southern scarce swallowtail

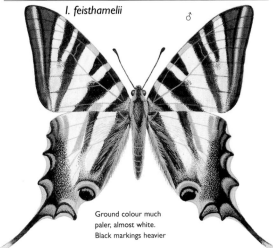

I. feisthamelii

♂

Ground colour much paler, almost white. Black markings heavier

This butterfly is often regarded as a subspecies of *I. podalirius*, but is larger and paler with difference between the broods. *WS:* 70–90 mm; *Flight:* Mar–Sept; *Gen:* 2; *FP:* as *I. podalirius*; *D:* Portugal, Spain, S France.

Southern festoon

Zerynthia polyxena

Small red spot present near forewing apex.
Marginal marks pronounced

Red patches on underside
vary in size

This species is easily confused with the Spanish festoon where their ranges overlap in southeast France. Identified by the absence of extensive red areas in the upper forewing, the Southern festoon is local in rocky regions up to 1000 m. *WS:* 46–52 mm; *Flight:* Apr–May; *Gen:* 1; *FP:* Birthwort (*Aristolochia*); *D:* Italy, Austria, SE France, Hungary, Romania, Yug, Bulgaria, Greece.

Spanish festoon

Z. rumina

Red spots in cell and
near apex

Vitreous window near
forewing apex

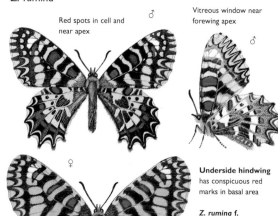

Underside hindwing
has conspicuous red
marks in basal area

***Z. rumina* f.
cantenera**, a common
female variant, is larger
and has a deep yellow
ground colour

Early to appear, the Spanish festoon is a variable-patterned butterfly, locally common on rough slopes up to 1500 m. Many subspecies are listed. *WS:* 44–46 mm; *Flight:* Feb–May; *Gen:* 1; *FP:* Birthwort (*Aristolochia*); *D:* SE France, Spain, Portugal.

Eastern festoon

Z. cerisyi

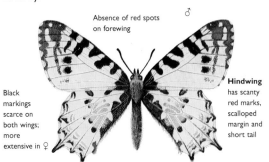

Absence of red spots on forewing

♂

Black markings scarce on both wings; more extensive in ♀

Hindwing has scanty red marks, scalloped margin and short tail

Flying over rough ground up to 1400 m, the Eastern festoon can be distinguished from other festoons by the lack of any red on the forewings and its scalloped hindwings. In Crete it is paler and smaller. *WS:* 52–62 mm; *Flight:* Apr–June; *Gen:* 1; *FP:* Birthwort (*Aristolochia*); *D:* Albania, Yug, Bulgaria, Greece, Crete.

False apollo

Archon apollinus

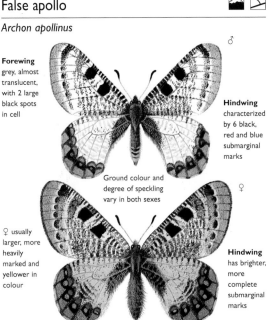

♂

Forewing grey, almost translucent, with 2 large black spots in cell

Hindwing characterized by 6 black, red and blue submarginal marks

Ground colour and degree of speckling vary in both sexes

♀

♀ usually larger, more heavily marked and yellower in colour

Hindwing has brighter, more complete submarginal marks

In flight, the False apollo looks yellower than most other festoons. Found in isolated colonies in rocky areas up to 1500 m, this species, which is widespread in Asia, occurs only in the extreme southeast of Europe. *WS:* 54–60 mm; *Flight:* Mar–Apr; *Gen:* 1; *FP:* Birthwort (*Aristolochia*); *D:* Bulgaria, Greece.

Apollo

Parnassius apollo

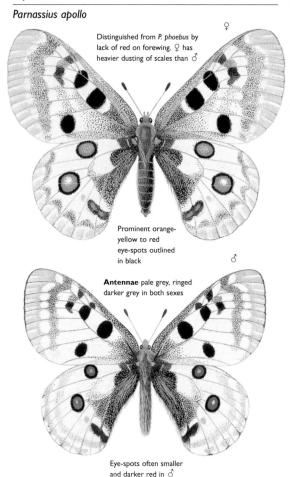

♀

Distinguished from *P. phoebus* by lack of red on forewing. ♀ has heavier dusting of scales than ♂

Prominent orange-yellow to red eye-spots outlined in black

♂

Antennae pale grey, ringed darker grey in both sexes

Eye-spots often smaller and darker red in ♂

The very distinctive pattern of the Apollo is prone to variation, and consequently many subspecies from different localities have been listed which all differ slightly in colour and markings. This large butterfly has a rather heavy, flapping flight which makes it easy prey for collectors. Due to its increasing rarity over recent years, there are now laws prohibiting the collection of the Apollo in several countries, as well as restrictions on trading in specimens. In Europe the Apollo is widely distributed, occurring in isolated colonies on mountainous regions from 700 to 2000 m. It may be distinguished from the related Small apollo (p 27) by the absence of red spots on the forewings and the much lighter dusting of dark scales, which gives it a white appearance. *WS:* 70–85 mm; *Flight:* June–Sept; *Gen:* usually 1; *FP:* Stonecrop (*Sedum*); *D:* Europe (not Britain, NW France, Denmark, N Scand, C Germany, Czech, Corsica, Sardinia).

Small apollo

P. phoebus

♂

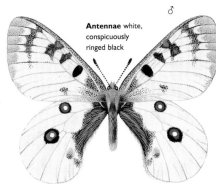

Antennae white, conspicuously ringed black

Fwing spotted red; black spot near hind margin much smaller than corresponding mark on Apollo

Ground colour yellow-white rather than pure white

At first glance the pattern of the Small apollo resembles that of the Apollo (p 26), but closer study reveals that it has more red on its forewings. Localized and comparatively rare, it occurs in small colonies on mountains over 2000 m, often by streams. The female is greyer with heavier markings. *WS:* 60–80 mm; *Flight:* July–Aug; *Gen:* 1; *FP:* Yellow saxifrage (*Saxifrage aizoides*), Mountain houseleek (*Sempervivum montanum*); *D:* Alps.

Clouded apollo

P. mnemosyne

♂

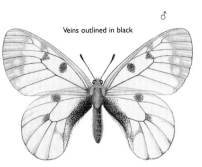

Veins outlined in black

Forewing poorly marked with only 2 black spots

Uppers lack any red spots and are dusted with black scales, often giving a very grey appearance

The absence of any red marks on either wing separates this species from other apollos. The female is similar to the male but for a heavier dusting of black scales. The clouded apollo prefers wooded hills up to 1500 m in central Europe, but further north it is considered to be a lowland species of damp meadows. There is some variation in pattern over its range. Specimens from Greece, *P. mnemosyne athene*, are both paler and smaller, while the female, *f. melaina*, found in more mountainous terrain, has more extensive black markings on its upperside. The butterfly has a flapping flight and is locally common in central Europe, but in Norway it is very rare and occurs in only a few localities. *WS:* 52–62 mm; *Flight:* May–July; *Gen:* 1; *FP:* Corydalis (*Corydalis*); *D:* Pyrenees, C and S France, Italy, Sicily, Alps, C and S Germany, Scand, Yug, Romania, Bulgaria, Greece, Poland, Czech, Switz (not Britain, Denmark, Spain, Portugal).

Whites and Yellows Pieridae

Some of the most common European butterflies belong to this family. They are easily recognized by their white or yellow black-spotted wings, and the caterpillars are generally green and smooth. The adults have six legs of equal size, each of which ends in four claws instead of the normal two. Many are strongly migratory, travelling long distances. The sexes and various generations usually differ.

Large white

Pieris brassicae

♀ 1st generation

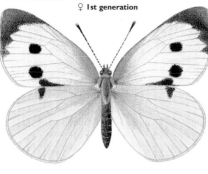

Black or grey-black apex

Forewing marked by 2 black spots and a black bar near hind margin

Hindwing pale yellow with single spot near front edge; **underside** dusted with grey scales

♂ 1st generation

Forewing unmarked but for black apex; **underside** has 2 black spots

Hindwing whiter, with less prominent spot near front edge than in ♀

Capable of completely stripping a cabbage of its leaves, the caterpillars of the Large or Cabbage white can be a serious garden pest. The resident population in Britain is fairly small, the numbers being increased each year by migrants coming in from Europe. Specimens from the summer generation are larger with more black on the wing tips than those seen in spring and autumn. *WS:* 57–66 mm; *Flight:* Apr–Oct; *Gen:* 2–3; *FP:* Cruciferae, esp Cabbage (*Brassica*); *D:* Europe.

Great southern white, *Ascia monuste*. is an American species, similar to the Large white, but has black triangles on wing veins at the margin and no black spots on the forewing. Female dimorphic; like male or with grey suffusion. *WS:* 44–57 mm; *Flight:* summer; *D:* migratory; accidental France.

African migrant

Catopsilia florella

This African species occasionally appears in southern and central Europe. *WS:* 54-56 mm; *Flight:* most months; *Gen:* 2 or more; *FP:* Cassia; *D:* Africa S of Sahara, Egypt, Tenerife, Canary Islands, India, China.

Male upperside almost unmarked; (female is whiter with darker fwing margin)

Small black marks on underside of fwing margin

Small white

Pieris rapae

♂ 1st generation

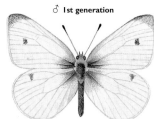

Forewing has small, greyish marks, poorly defined; more distinct on underside

Hindwing unmarked but for small black spot towards front edge

♀ 1st generation

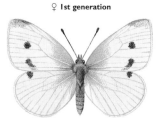

Ground colour pale yellow with extensive dusting of grey scales in basal area

Spots are more clearly defined than in 1st gen ♂. The 2nd generation is normally darker and more heavily marked

The favourite haunt of the Small white, one of the most common British butterflies, is likely to be the cabbage rows of market gardens, although it may be found in a variety of habitats, from urban parks to open countryside. It is noticeably smaller but more numerous than the Large white, and feeds on a greater variety of plants. The resident British population is augmented each year by large numbers from abroad. *WS:* 46–55 mm; *Flight:* Mar–Sept; *Gen:* 2–3; *FP:* Cruciferae, esp Wild mignonette (*Reseda lutea*), Cabbage (*Brassica*); *D:* Europe (less common in N Scand).

Southern small white

Pieris mannii

♂

Forewing apical spot usually extends further down wing margin than in *P. rapae*.

Underside hindwing yellow, dusted with black scales

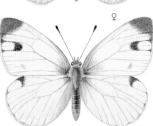

♀

Forewing apical spot broader, blacker than in ♂; crescent-shaped spot linked to margin by dark scales along the veins

Hindwing costal spot outwardly concave

This is smaller than the Small white (p 29). It flies over cultivated land, but fortunately the caterpillars feed only on wild Cruciferae. Later generations are larger and darker. *WS:* 40–46 mm; *Flight:* Mar–Sept; *Gen:* 3–4; *FP:* Evergreen candytuft (*Iberis sempervirens*); *D:* Spain, France, Switz, Austria, Italy, SE Europe.

Mountain small white

P. ergane

Forewing dark apical spot is rather square

Underside fwing unmarked except for yellow apex

Hindwing small grey costal mark often absent

♂

♀

Forewing has additional black spot in ♀

Hindwing pale yellow with larger costal spot than ♂

Dark spots on uppers may show through on the underside

Later generations are darker

One of the smaller, less common whites in Europe, found on grassy mountain slopes up to 1800 m. *WS:* 36–48 mm; *Flight:* Mar–Sept; *Gen:* 2 or more; *FP:* Cruciferae, esp Burnt candytuft (*Aethionema saxatile*); *D:* NE Spain, S France, Italy (Apennines), Romania, Hungary, Yug, Albania, Bulgaria, Greece.

Green-veined white

P. napi

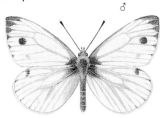

♂

Grey triangles at each vein

Veins dusted with grey scales

Veins lined green

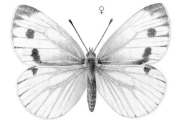

♀

Markings better-defined in ♀

Underside hwing yellow, less heavily veined

A. napi radiata f. sulphurea, a rare form, found in Ireland

♂

Bright lemon-yellow ground colour with dark veins

This is a variable species and several very similar, related species can all be called by the name Green-veined white. Distinct differences do occur between spring and summer generations, the latter being larger with paler veins. Unfortunately, this species, which is not a garden pest, may be mistaken for the much more harmful Small white, as they both fly over similar terrain. However, the Green-veined white prefers damp meadows up to 1500 m. *P. adalwinda* is the Scandinavian Green-veined white; *P. blanca* is the Green-veined white of former Yug. *WS:* 36–50 mm; *Flight:* May–Sept; *Gen:* 2 or more; *FP:* Cruciferae, esp Wild mignonette (*Reseda lutea*), Hedge mustard (*Sisymbrium officinale*); *D:* Europe (rare in N Scand).

Mountain green-veined white, *Pieris bryoniae*, is often considered a subspecies of *P. napi*, but there is considerable variation between specimens. The black veins are prominent on the upperside which often has a dusky suffusion on the forewing. *WS:* 38–48 mm; *Flight:* June-Aug; *Gen:* 1, *FP:* Cruciferae; *D:* SE Europe generally in Alps, Tatra and Carpathians.

Krueper's small white

Pieris krueperi ♂

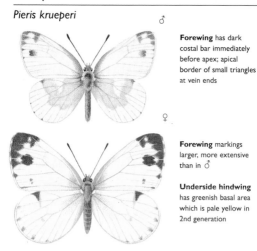

Forewing has dark costal bar immediately before apex; apical border of small triangles at vein ends

♀

Forewing markings larger, more extensive than in ♂

Underside hindwing has greenish basal area which is pale yellow in 2nd generation

Krueper's small white is widespread in rocky areas up to 2000 m and may be separated from the Mountain small white (p 30) by its distinctive apical forewing marks and the greenish basal area underneath the hindwing. Closer inspection of the upper hindwing margin will also reveal a row of small grey marks, but these are barely visible in some specimens. *WS:* 45–50 mm; *Flight:* Mar–Sept; *Gen:* 2 or more; *FP:* Mountain alison (*Alyssum montanum*); *D:* Greece, Bulgaria, Yug.

Black-veined white

Aporia crataegi ♂

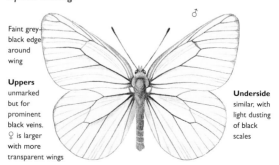

Faint grey-black edge around wing

Uppers unmarked but for prominent black veins. ♀ is larger with more transparent wings

Underside similar, with light dusting of black scales

This distinctive butterfly is usually seen flying in its rather laboured fashion over clover fields and in orchards, where it can be a pest if numerous. The population fluctuates drastically from year to year, and a good year may see an occasional migrant to Britain, which arouses great interest as the British population became extinct some 60 years ago. *WS:* 56–68 mm; *Flight:* May–June; *Gen:* 1; *FP:* Hawthorn (*Crataegus*), Cherry, Blackthorn (*Prunus*) and others; *D:* Europe (migrant to Britain, N Scand).

Bath white

Pieris daplidice

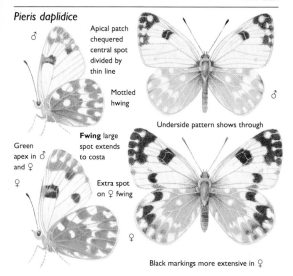

♂

Apical patch chequered central spot divided by thin line

Mottled hwing

♂

Underside pattern shows through

Green apex in ♂ and ♀

♀

Fwing large spot extends to costa

Extra spot on ♀ fwing

♀

Black markings more extensive in ♀

A rare migrant to southern Britain, this species derives its name from an eighteenth-century embroidery made in Bath, in which it is clearly shown. It has a rapid flight and may be seen bobbing around in clover fields. *WS:* 42–48 mm; *Flight:* Feb–Sept; *Gen:* 2–3; *FP:* Cruciferae, esp Rock cress (*Arabis*), Mustard (*Sinapis*); *D:* C and S Europe (migrant to Britain, Holland, Scand).

Small Bath white

P. chloridice

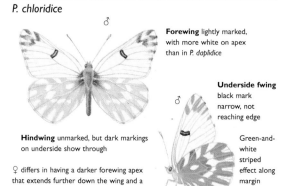

♂

Forewing lightly marked, with more white on apex than in *P. daplidice*

Underside fwing black mark narrow, not reaching edge

♂

Green-and-white striped effect along margin

Hindwing unmarked, but dark markings on underside show through

♀ differs in having a darker forewing apex that extends further down the wing and a series of small marginal marks on hindwing

A smaller and more lightly marked butterfly than the Bath white, the Small Bath white is confined to the mountains of southeastern Europe, being more widespread in central Asia. The second generation is larger than the first and the upperside markings are better developed. *WS:* 40–44 mm; *Flight:* Apr–June; *Gen:* 2; *FP:* unknown; *D:* Bulgaria, Albania, Turkey, Greece.

Peak white

Pieris callidice

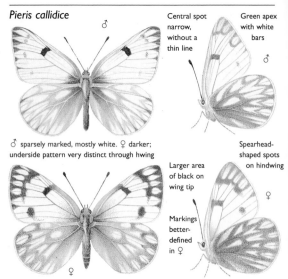

Central spot narrow, without a thin line

Green apex with white bars

♂ sparsely marked, mostly white. ♀ darker; underside pattern very distinct through hwing

Spearhead-shaped spots on hindwing

Larger area of black on wing tip

Markings better-defined in ♀

The Peak white is a butterfly of mountains and Alpine valleys from 1500 up to 3000 m. It closely resembles the Bath white and the Small Bath white, differing most noticeably in the shape of the markings on the green underside of the hindwing. In the male these spearhead-shaped marks are white, while in the female they are yellowish. Although there is usually only one generation, a second may occur at lower altitudes in August if conditions are favourable. *WS:* 42–42 mm; *Flight:* June–July; *Gen:* 1–2; *FP:* Dwarf treacle mustard (*Erysimum pumilum*), Mignonette (*Reseda*), other Cruciferae; *D:* Pyrenees and Alps (NE Spain, France, Switz, Austria, N Italy).

Desert orange tip

Colotis evagore

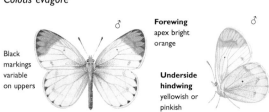

Black markings variable on uppers

Forewing apex bright orange

Underside hindwing yellowish or pinkish

Far more common in Africa than in Europe, the Desert orange tip has extended its range to include a pocket in southern Spain. This is a smaller, more delicate butterfly than the Orange tip (p 36), with less orange on its wings. The female is similar to the male but for a narrower orange patch, while later generations are smaller and paler. *WS:* 30–36 mm; *Flight:* Feb–Aug; *Gen:* several; *FP:* Caper (*Capparis spinosa*); *D:* S Spain.

Dappled white

Euchloe simplonia

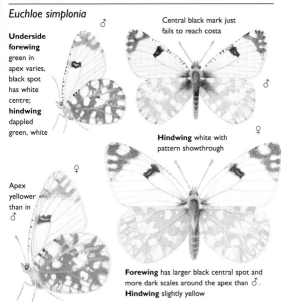

Underside forewing green in apex varies, black spot has white centre; **hindwing** dappled green, white

♂

Central black mark just fails to reach costa

♂

♀

Hindwing white with pattern showthrough

♀

Apex yellower than in ♂

Forewing has larger black central spot and more dark scales around the apex than ♂. **Hindwing** slightly yellow

A widespread butterfly on grassy slopes up to 1400 m, with many subspecies based on small differences in pattern. *WS:* 40–48 mm; *Flight:* Mar–June; *Gen:* 2; *FP:* Cruciferae, esp Candytuft (*Iberis*); *D:* Spain, Portugal, C and S France, Italy, Switz, SE Europe.
E. ausonia (Mountain dappled white) is distinguished by the black spot on the forewing which actually reaches the costa and spreads along it. Flies over mountains from 1500 to 2000 m. *WS:* 40–48 mm; *Flight:* June; *Gen:* 1; *D:* Pyrenees, Alps, Yug.

Portuguese dappled white

E. tagis

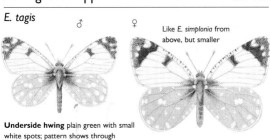

♂ ♀

Like *E. simplonia* from above, but smaller

Underside hwing plain green with small white spots; pattern shows through

The underside hindwing is green with a few white spots. Found in rough meadows up to 1000 m. *WS:* 30–44 mm; *Flight:* Feb–May; *Gen:* 1; *FP:* Candytuft (*Iberis*); *D:* Spain, Portugal, S France.
E. belemia (Green-striped white) is similar but with white stripes running across the green underside hindwing. *WS:* 36–44 mm; *Flight:* Feb–May; *Gen:* 2; *FP:* Candytuft (*Iberis*), Hedge Mustard (*Sisymbrium*); *D:* S Spain, Portugal.

35

Greenish black tip

Euchloe charlonia

♂

Uppers lime yellow in both sexes with a broad black patch at the forewing apex

♀ has larger black spot in cell of forewing

Strictly speaking this is an African butterfly, but the subspecies *E. charlonia penia* is found in a few isolated rocky places in Europe and is larger than its North African counterparts. *WS: 32–36 mm; Flight:* Apr–June; *Gen:* 2; *FP: Matthiola tessala;* D: SE Yug, N Greece, Bulgaria.

Orange tip

Anthocharis cardamines

♂

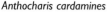

♂

Extreme tip is black

Apex dappled green and white

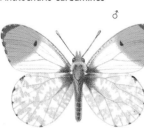

Forewing large orange patch on outer third just encloses small black spot.
Hindwing dappled grey-green effect caused by underside pattern

Underside hindwing mottled green and white in ♂ and ♀

Forewing lacks orange patch, central spot bigger, often crescent-shaped; **underside** white, poorly marked, with grey apex

♀

Grey apex does not have any distinct white spots; this distinguishes it from *E. simplonia*
Hindwing may have yellow tinge

Common in damp meadows, woodland edges and country lanes, the Orange tip is the only species in Britain with a distinctive dappled-green underside. This coloration is a peculiar effect of the mixing of black and yellow scales, and serves as a useful camouflage. Occasionally drawn to the ornamental Cruciferae of urban parks, the sight of this butterfly is thought by many to be a true sign of spring. *WS: 39–48 mm; Flight:* Apr–July; *Gen:* 1; *FP:* Cruciferae, esp Tower mustard (*Arabis glabra*), Lady's smock (*Cardamine pratensis*); D: Europe (not N Scand, N Scot).
A. gruneri (Gruner's orange tip) is smaller with a pale yellow ground colour. *WS: 30–36 mm; Flight:* Mar–May; *FP: Aethionema saxatilis;* D: Greece, Albania, SE Yug, Turkey.

Moroccan orange tip

A. euphenoides

♂

Underside hwing
yellow with greenish
patches and a row
of white postdiscal
spots

♂

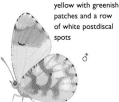

Uppers yellow
with broad orange
band on forewing

Orange-grey apex

Uppers white
with black spot on
fwing larger, not
enclosed by
orange areas
as in ♂

Hindwing flushed
pale yellow

♀

There are two closely related species, of which *A. euphenoides* occurs
in Europe while the similar *A. belia* appears to be restricted to
N Africa. Usually found in mountainous regions up to 2000 m, it
is sometimes mistaken for the Eastern orange tip, even though
their ranges do not overlap. The latter has a bolder underside
hindwing pattern. *WS:* 36–40 mm; *Flight:* May–July; *Gen:* 1;
FP: Buckler mustard (*Biscutella laevigata*); *D:* Spain, Portugal,
S France, Italy, Switz.

Eastern orange tip

A. damone

Uppers similar to
A. euphensoides

Underside hindwing
strongly mottled green
and yellow, in irregular
pattern like that of
A. cardamines

♂

Uppers white, lacking
orange patch near
forewing apex

Underside markings
as in ♂

♀

Very little is known about this local orange tip, which may be
found flying on rocky mountain slopes up to 1000 m. *WS:* 38–40
mm; *Flight:* Apr–June; *Gen:* 1; *FP:* Woad (*Isatis tinctoria*); *D:*
Sicily, S Italy, Greece, SE Yug.

Sooty orange tip

Zegris eupheme

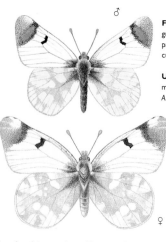

♂

Forewing apical area grey-green enclosing small orange patch; central black mark curved

Underside hindwing yellow, marbled grey-green as in *A. euphenoides*

Forewing orange patch smaller than in ♂, often absent; **underside** apex yellow in both sexes

♀ often larger than ♂

♀

Very local in southern Europe, this species has a fast flight which carries it over rough flowery slopes up to 1000 m. At lower altitudes in southern Spain it may be on the wing as early as April, becoming later with increasing altitude. *WS:* 46–50 mm; *Flight:* Apr–June; *Gen:* 1; *FP:* Horay mustard (*Sinapis incana*); *D:* S Spain, S Portugal.

Mountain clouded yellow

Colias phicomone

♂

Forewing row of pale submarginal spots stands out against dark border

Uppers yellowish-green with heavy dusting of grey scales

Hindwing darker, bright spot visible from underside

Uppers paler, whitish-green but otherwise similar to ♂; amount of grey variable

Underside hindwing bright yellow in both sexes with clear orange central spot

♀

Found on Alpine meadows from 2000 m upwards, this species occasionally produces a second brood in September. *WS:* 40–50 mm; *Flight:* June–Aug; *Gen:* 1; *FP:* Leguminosae, esp Vicia; *D:* Spain (Cantabrians, Pyrenees), Switz, Austria, S France (Alps).

Moorland clouded yellow

C. palaeno

Uppers lemon-yellow; unbroken black border

♂

White spot on fwing has dark edge

Black border narrower on hindwing. Both wings fringed in red

Underside forewing white with yellow apex

♀

♀

Underside hindwing yellow with grey-green dust

Uppers white with markings as in ♂, but less clearly defined. **Hindwing** dusted grey, small spot appearing on both sides in ♂ and ♀

Several subspecies based on small differences in colour and pattern have been described. The Moorland clouded yellow is a strong flyer, found in lowland bogs. *WS:* 48–64 mm; *Flight:* June–July; *Gen:* 1; *FP:* Bog whortleberry (*Vaccinium uliginosum*); *D:* Scand, NE France, Germany, Poland, Czech, Alps.

Pale Arctic clouded yellow

C. nastes

Uppers lemon-yellow without heavy dusting of dark scales

Wing fringes usually red

Hindwing tiny round yellow spot near centre

The Pale Arctic clouded yellow is, as its name suggests, strictly an Arctic species, and for this reason is unlikely to be mistaken in the field for the Mountain clouded yellow (p 38), which only flies in the Pyrenees and Alps. The female is whiter with more grey scales on the hindwing. Found on mountainous moorland above 400 m. *WS:* 44–48 mm; *Flight:* June–July; *Gen:* 1; *FP:* Alpine milk vetch (*Astragalus alpinus*); *D:* N Scand.

Lesser clouded yellow

Colias chrysotheme ♂

Forewing central spot small, often reddish. Dark wing borders crossed by yellow veins

Underside yellow with row of black postdiscal spots on both wings

The female is close in appearance to the female Danube clouded yellow, except that the more pointed forewing has a broad, greenish-grey costal margin. Flies over grassland up to 1000 m. *WS:* 40–48 mm; *Flight:* May–Aug; *Gen:* 2; *FP:* Hairy tare (*Vicia hirsuta*); *D:* Austria, Hungary, Romania, Czech.

Danube clouded yellow

C. myrmidone

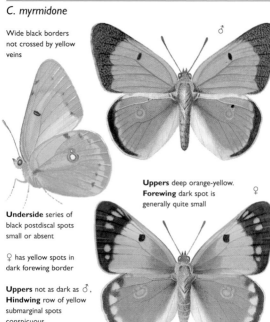

Wide black borders not crossed by yellow veins

♂

Underside series of black postdiscal spots small or absent

♀ has yellow spots in dark forewing border

Uppers not as dark as ♂, **Hindwing** row of yellow submarginal spots conspicuous

greenish white ♀s also exist

Uppers deep orange-yellow. **Forewing** dark spot is generally quite small

♀

The main features to look out for when identifying this species are deep orange uppers and the apparent lack of venation on the wing borders. It has the typical fast flight of the clouded yellows and is found mainly in the Danube basin. *WS:* 44–50 mm; *Flight:* May–Aug; *Gen:* 2; *FP:* Broom (*Cytisus*); *D:* Romania, Hungary, S Germany, Czech, Austria, Bulgaria, Yug.

Balkan clouded yellow

C. balcanica

Deeper in colour
and with a duskier
hindwing than *C.
myrmidone*; otherwise
similar

Pale submarginal marks
along the inside of the
dark hindwing border
are slightly more
noticeable

This is a very local species which is associated with the open wood-land of the Balkan mountain range. The female of this species is larger and darker than the female Danube clouded yellow. *WS:* 50–54 mm; *Flight:* July–Aug; *Gen:* 1; *FP:* unknown; *D:* Yug, Bulgaria (not Greece).

Greek clouded yellow

C. aurorina

Uppers dark orange
with black border
crossed by yellow veins

Very pale purple reflection
on wing at certain angles

Underside dull yellow-green, with red-edged
spot on hindwing

Black border broken
by fairly large spots
which form a regular
series on hindwing

Underside hindwing
pale grey-green with
small white central spot

Like many of the other clouded yellows, the females may vary in colour, with some rare forms almost white. The pale purple sheen on the male upperside is an attractive and characteristic feature of this species. It occurs locally on mountain slopes from 1600 to 2600 m. *WS:* 54–56 mm; *Flight:* June–July; *Gen:* 1; *FP:* Milk vetch (*Astragalus*); *D:* Greece.

Clouded yellow

Colias crocea

♂

Uppers
bright orange-
yellow with
broad black
margins
crossed by
yellow veins

Underside
yellow with
green tinge
on forewing
margin and
all over
hindwing

♀

**Differs from
♂ in having
wider black
margins
enclosing
yellow spots
of uneven size**

Hindwing
dusky with
prominent
orange spots

♀

Underside forewing
black postdiscal spots are
larger than in ♂

♀

C. crocea f. helice,
a ♀ form, has pale
green-white uppers
with grey suffusion
over hindwings

Twin orange spots on
upper hindwing are
white with red edge
on underside
(♂ and ♀)

The Clouded yellow is a powerful, fast-flying butterfly which is
strongly migratory and may appear anywhere in Europe except for
the more northerly areas of Scandinavia. Unable to survive the
northern winter, the British population depends each year on fresh
migrations from the Mediterranean, the first butterflies usually
arriving in late May. These migrants breed to produce a 'native'
generation in August and September and are more commonly seen
along the south coast. The Clouded yellow prefers open spaces,
and is attracted to fields of clover or lucerne. *WS:* 45–54 mm;
Flight: Apr–Sept: *Gen:* several; *FP:* Birdsfoot trefoil (*Lotis corniculatus*), Lucerne (*Medicago sativa*), Clover (*Trigolium*), *D:* Europe
(migrant to Britain, Holland, S Scand).

Northern clouded yellow

C. hecla
♂

Uppers orange-yellow with dark, wing borders crossed by yellow veins and dusted with yellow scales on forewing

Underside grey-green except for pale orange-yellow discal area in forewing

♀

Forewing paler than ♂ with dark veins and yellow-green spots in margin

Hindwing dusted with grey scales; submarginal spots in regular series

Locally common up to 1000 m, the Northern clouded yellow is probably circumpolar, occurring in Arctic Europe and N America. White females are unknown. *WS:* 40–46 mm; *Flight:* June–July; *Gen:* 1; *FP:* Alpine milk vetch (*Astragalus alpinus*); *D:* N Scand.

Pale clouded yellow

C. hyale
♂

Uppers pale yellow with spots in forewing border

♂

♀

Underside hindwing golden yellow with white, red-edged spot shaped like figure of 8. ♀ white with slight green tint; otherwise similar to ♂

Hindwing lacks grey suffusion, distinguishing it from ♀ *C. crocea*

Originates in southern Europe and migrates northwards, feeding on clover. Probably replaced in Italy and Spain by *C. alfacariensis* (p 44). A rare migrant to Britain. *WS:* 42–50 mm; *Flight:* May–Sept; *Gen:* 2–3; *FP:* Clover (*Trifolium*); *D:* Europe (not N Scand).

43

Berger's clouded yellow

Colias alfacariensis

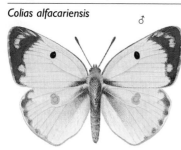

♂

Distinguished from very similar *C. hyale* by brighter, lemon-yellow ground colour

Hindwing has large, bright orange central spot and narrow dark margin.

♀ greenish-white, pattern as in ♂; difficult to separate from ♀ *C. hyale*

The range of this species is uncertain because of its similarity to *C. hyale* (p 43). The latter prefers lucerne fields while Berger's clouded yellow is more common on downs. *WS:* 42–54 mm. *Flight:* May–Sept; *Gen:* 2; *FP:* Horseshoe vetch (*Hippocrepis comosa*); *D:* W and C Europe (not Scand; migrant to S Britain, Holland). *C. erate* (Eastern pale clouded yellow) is yellow with unbroken dark borders in the male. *WS:* 46–52 mm; *D:* SE Europe.

Cleopatra

Gonepteryx cleopatra

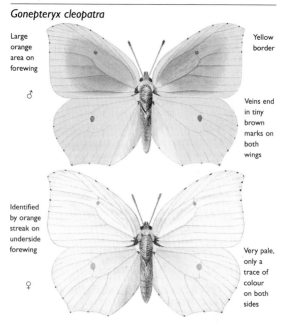

Large orange area on forewing

♂

Yellow border

Veins end in tiny brown marks on both wings

Identified by orange streak on underside forewing

♀

Very pale, only a trace of colour on both sides

Cleopatra is a rapid flyer, similar in shape and colouring to the commoner Brimstone (p 45). It overwinters in the adult form and is locally common on open, lightly wooded slopes. There are several subspecies. *WS:* 50–68 mm; *Flight:* Feb–Aug; *Gen:* 1; *FP:* Buckthorn (*Rhamnus*); *D:* Spain, S France, Italy, Greece, Yug.

G. rhamni

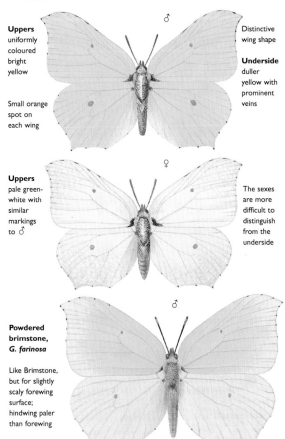

♂

Uppers uniformly coloured bright yellow

Small orange spot on each wing

Distinctive wing shape

Underside duller yellow with prominent veins

♀

Uppers pale green-white with similar markings to ♂

The sexes are more difficult to distinguish from the underside

♂

Powdered brimstone, G. farinosa

Like Brimstone, but for slightly scaly forewing surface; hindwing paler than forewing

In Britain, any bright yellow butterfly seen in early spring is likely to be a male brimstone. The female usually emerges later and can be mistaken for a white, but the leaf-like shape of the wing identifies her. It is possible that the Brimstone was once known as the 'butter-coloured fly' and that the contracted form gave rise to the word 'butterfly'. The species has a powerful flight and is common in woods, gardens and roadsides up to 2000 m. It is one of the few butterflies to hibernate in the adult form, hiding in evergreen plants such as ivy, where its closed wings provide an effective camouflage. *WS:* 52–60 mm; *Flight:* July–Sept (hibernated specimens appear in April to lay eggs); *Gen:* 1; *FP:* Buckthorn (*Rhamnus*), Alder buckthorn (*R. frangula*); *D:* Europe (not N Scand, Scot).

Powdered brimstone, *G. farinosa*, is rarer, and found on mountains. *WS:* 56–64 mm; *Flight:* May–June; *Gen:* 1; *FP:* Buckthorn (*Rhamnus*); *D:* SE Europe.

Wood white

Leptidea sinapis

1st generation

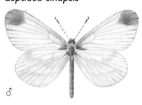

♂

Apical spot reduced to grey
streaks along veins

Smaller, more fragile than the other whites, the Wood white may be found flying close to the ground in forest clearings and woodland edges. The second generation is whiter with smaller but blacker apical spots. *WS:* 36–48 mm; *Flight:* May–Aug; *Gen:* 2 or more; *FP:* Everlasting pea (*Lathyrus*), Birdsfoot trefoil (*Lotus*); *D:* Europe (not Scot, Holland, Denmark, N Scand).

Eastern wood white

L. duponcheli

♂

1st generation ♀

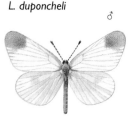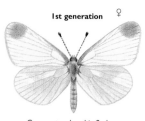

Wings slightly pointed, tinged yellow

Grey spot reduced in 2nd gen

The antennal clubs of this species are dark underneath, unlike those of the Wood white which have a white mark. Flies over open slopes. *WS:* 34–42 mm; *Flight:* Apr–Aug; *Gen:* 2; *FP:* Sainfoin (*Onobrychis viciifolia*); *D:* S France, SE Europe.

Fenton's wood white

L. morsei

Larger in size
than the other
wood whites

Apical spot
grey, rounded;
much smaller
in ♀

**2nd
generation**

Wings chalky
white on
both sides

♂

The antennal clubs are white underneath, as in the Wood white. It is also mainly a woodland species, with a typical weak flight. The first generation is usually greyer than the second. *WS:* 42–46 mm; *Flight:* Apr–July; *Gen:* 2; *FP:* Spring pea (*Lathyrus vernus*); *D:* Austria, Hungary, Romania, NW Yug.

Monarch butterflies Danaidae

Most of the species in this family occur in the tropics of Africa and southeast Asia, but a few originate in the New World continents of North and South America. The Monarch is famous for its remarkable annual migration from Mexico to Canada. Occasionally some migrants stray off-course and arrive in Europe, but there is some debate over whether these butterflies come from America or from the nearer Canary Islands. The adults tend to be large, brightly coloured butterflies with a powerful but unhurried flight. They are distasteful to predators and are extremely tough, being able to withstand the odd trial peck from a curious bird without shortening their adult life of 8 or 9 months. In both sexes the front legs are small and not used for walking.

Monarch caterpillar

Two pairs of long black horns at each end of smooth body

Toxins in foodplant are stored by caterpillar

Monarch

Danaus plexippus

Chestnut-brown wings with black veins; 2 rows of white spots in wide black borders

♂

The infrequent but regular occurrence of this large and beautiful butterfly in Europe often gives rise to much local interest. Unfortunately it is unable to breed in the wild in Europe because its foodplant does not grow here. However, in other parts of the world such as Australia, Java and the Philippines, the Monarch or Milkweed has successfully established itself by adapting to new foodplants. In America the butterflies move in large numbers and some of their winter tree roosts have become tourist attractions. *WS:* 75–100 mm; *Flight:* all year (late summer in Europe); *Gen:* several; *FP:* Milkweed (*Asclepias curassavica*); *D:* migrant to W Europe, including Britain.

D. chrysippus (Plain tiger) is an African species, similar in colouring but less marked. *WS:* 70–84 mm; *Flight:* summer; *D:* migrant to Mediterranean, esp Andalucia, Greece, S Italy.

Snout butterflies Libytheidae

This is a family of comparatively few species, with one in Europe, one in North America, and the rest in the Old World tropics of Africa and Asia. The butterflies tend to be small in size, and are characterized by the long palps that project in front of the head like a beak or snout, giving the family its popular name. The wing borders are serrated, with a prominent tooth on the forewing. Many species are migratory and of similar appearance, usually with a dark brown ground colour and orange markings. The forelegs are reduced in the male, as in the Nymphalidae, but in the female they are of normal length.

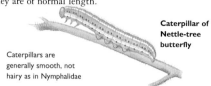

Caterpillar of Nettle-tree butterfly

Caterpillars are generally smooth, not hairy as in Nymphalidae

Nettle-tree butterfly

Libythea celtis

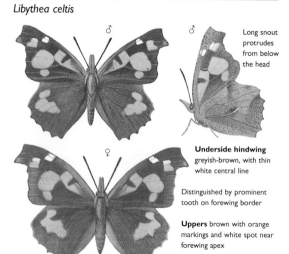

♂

♂

Long snout protrudes from below the head

Underside hindwing greyish-brown, with thin white central line

Distinguished by prominent tooth on forewing border

Uppers brown with orange markings and white spot near forewing apex

Sexes are similar

♀

There is very little variation in pattern in this species over its European range. Also known as the Beak butterfly, it may be found flying near its foodplant in light woodland areas up to 500 m, although in late summer occasional vagrants occur at much higher altitudes. The adults spend a long period in hibernation, from September until March, when they fly again to lay their eggs for the next generation. The distinctive toothing on the forewing border and the protruding snout easily distinguish it from other European butterflies. *WS:* 34–44 mm; *Flight:* Mar–Apr, June–Sept; *Gen:* 1; *FP:* Nettle tree (*Celtis australis*); *D:* Spain, Portugal, S France, Italy, Sicily, Austria, Romania, Yug, Bulgaria, Hungary, Greece, Corsica, Sardinia.

Brush-footed butterflies Nymphalidae

This family, the largest, has been divided into many subfamilies, with species occurring worldwide. They are medium to large, often brightly coloured, and include some of the most well-known butterflies, such as the tortoiseshells, admirals and peacocks. The adults in both sexes have reduced forelegs which are tucked up against the thorax, so that only four legs are used for walking. Dense tufts of scales are attached to these forelegs, especially in the male, which give a 'brush-footed' appearance. The caterpillars are usually spiny and striking, but vary considerably. Some, such as the Small tortoiseshell (p 57), live in large groups in silken webs.

Gregarious. Black spiny body speckled with white

Peacock caterpillar

Two-tailed pasha

Charaxes jasius

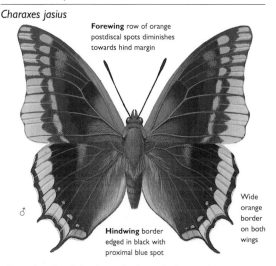

Forewing row of orange postdiscal spots diminishes towards hind margin

Wide orange border on both wings

♂

Hindwing border edged in black with proximal blue spot

The underside of this butterfly bears little resemblance to the upperside, being conspicuously marked with black spots and streaks outlined in white and set against a chocolate-brown ground colour. The two short tails on the hindwing are quite conspicuous, but usually it is the rapid and powerful flight that is first noticed. The Two-tailed pasha is the only representative in Europe of the widespread African group, with a range confined mainly to the coastal regions and islands of the Mediterranean. It rarely flies above 800 m and is very local in distribution. The female is larger than the male but otherwise similar in markings. *WS:* 76–83 mm; *Flight:* May–Sept; *Gen:* 2; *FP:* Strawberry tree (*Arbutus unedo*); *D:* Spain, Portugal, S France, Italy (west coast only), Greece, Yug, Albania, Corsica, Sardinia, Sicily.

Purple emperor

Apatura iris

♂

Forewing has obscure round black spot near middle of outer margin

Purple iridescence seen only from certain angles; otherwise wings appear brownish

♀

♀ not as dark as ♂ and lacking purple sheen

White markings larger than ♂

Considered to be a rare species, this large and beautiful butterfly has a powerful flight and is much sought-after by collectors. Elusive rather than rare would perhaps be a more apt description, as it spends most of its time in the tree tops, the males occasionally coming down to feed at damp patches such as sap, dung and carrion. The females seldom descend except to deposit their eggs on young willow trees. Well-established oakwoods up to 1000 m form their main breeding grounds, within which an adequate supply of foodplant must be found in order for them to survive. In Britain the species has only been recorded in the south and east. There is a recurrent rare form, f. *iole*, which lacks any white marks on its upperside. *WS:* 62–74 mm; *Flight:* July–Aug; *Gen:* 1; *FP:* Sallow (*Salix caprea*), Grey willow (*S. cinerea*); *D:* Europe (not Italy, Balkans, Norway, Sweden).

Lesser purple emperor

A. ilia

Uppers similar to
A. iris, except for
orange-ringed black
spot on forewing

Hindwing white
discal band has wavy
inside edge

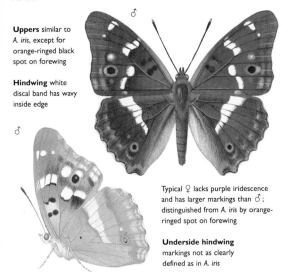

♂

Typical ♀ lacks purple iridescence
and has larger markings than ♂;
distinguished from A. iris by orange-
ringed spot on forewing

Underside hindwing
markings not as clearly
defined as in A. iris

♀

**A. ilia f.
clytie** has pale
yellow-brown
markings on
uppers in ♂
and ♀, except
for white
apical spots on
forewing

Both sexes occur in two distinct forms in most localities; the 'typical' dark brown form which resembles the Purple emperor (p 50)
and the yellowish-brown form, f. *clytie*. There are also several subspecies which vary slightly in pattern. *A. ilia barcina*, for example,
has more extensive white markings. The Lesser purple emperor is
a widespread woodland species, with similar habits to the Purple
emperor. *WS:* 64–70 mm; *Flight:* May–June, Aug–Sept; *Gen:* 2
(1 in north); *FP:* Poplar (*Pupulus*), Willow (*Salix*); *D:* Europe (not
Britain, Holland, Scand).
A. metis (Freyer's purple emperor) is similar but smaller, and its
upper hindwing lacks a broad dark postdiscal band. Rare. *WS:*
60–64 mm; *Flight, Gen, FP:* as above; *D:* SE Europe.

51

Poplar admiral

Limenitis populi

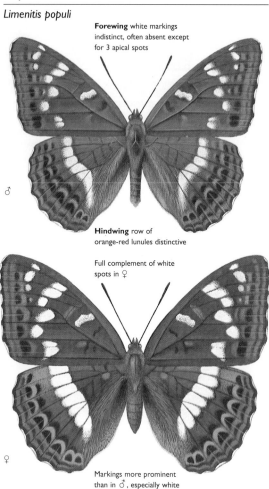

Forewing white markings indistinct, often absent except for 3 apical spots

Hindwing row of orange-red lunules distinctive

Full complement of white spots in ♀

♂

♀

Markings more prominent than in ♂, especially white discal band on hindwing

Although the female has more white on the upperside than the male, it still has comparatively less than the White admiral (p 53). The row of orange-red, crescent-shaped marks on the hindwing is also diagnostic. During the day this butterfly is active in the tree tops, but the pungent smell of carrion or dung will often attract it down to the ground. Open woodland, especially along the edges of streams where poplars grow, is the preferred habitat, where it is most likely to be seen early in the day. The bright orange underside with white bands and dark spots contrasts markedly with the dark brown upperside. *WS:* 70–80 mm; *Flight:* June–Aug; *Gen:* 1; *FP:* Poplar (*Populus*), esp Aspen (*P. tremula*); *D:* C and E Europe (rare in W France, Denmark, Holland; absent from Spain, Portugal, Britain, peninsular Italy, Greece, N Scand).

Southern white admiral

L. reducta

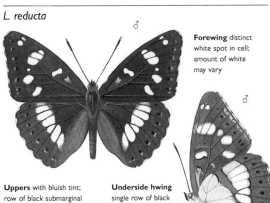

♂

Forewing distinct white spot in cell; amount of white may vary

♂

Uppers with bluish tint; row of black submarginal spots edged in blue on both wings

Underside hwing single row of black submarginal spots

Distinguished from the White admiral by the single row of black spots on the hindwing underside and the central white spot on the forewing. It flies slowly and gracefully in lightly wooded areas, feeding at flowers with its wings outspread. The sexes are similar. *WS:* 46–54 mm; *Flight:* May–Sept; *Gen:* 2; *FP:* Honeysuckle (*Lonicera periclymenum*); *D:* S and C Europe (rare in N and W France; absent from Britain, Holland, N Germany, Scand).

White admiral

L. camilla

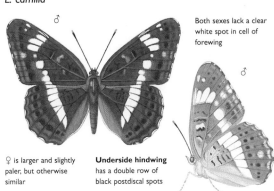

♂

Both sexes lack a clear white spot in cell of forewing

♂

♀ is larger and slightly paler, but otherwise similar

Underside hindwing has a double row of black postdiscal spots

The White admiral has a slow, measured flight, sometimes gliding, and is locally common in woodland glades, where it feeds freely on blackberry blossom. In Britain its range in the south seems to be increasing, most noticeably in the Forest of Dean. Generally it occurs singly, but sometimes numbers may congregate in shady places, especially when feeding. *WS:* 52–60 mm; *Flight:* June–July; *Gen:* 1; *FP:* Honeysuckle (*Lonicera periclymenum*); *D:* C Europe, including S Britain, S Sweden (not Ireland, Norway, Finland, S Italy).

Common glider

Neptis sappho

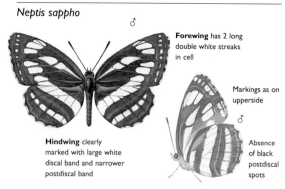

♂

Forewing has 2 long double white streaks in cell

Markings as on upperside

♂

Absence of black postdiscal spots

Hindwing clearly marked with large white discal band and narrower postdiscal band

The flight is steady with, as its name implies, a gliding as well as a flapping movement. It flies in woodlands and shrub-covered hillsides at low altitudes, and is commonly associated with Fenton's wood white (p 46), as they both share the same foodplant and distribution. The female is similar to the male and is readily distinguished from the Hungarian glider by the presence of two transverse white bands on the upper hindwing. Also popularly known as the Common sailor. *WS:* 44–48 mm; *Flight:* May–June, July–Sept; *Gen:* 2; *FP:* Spring pea (*Lathyrus vernus*); *D:* lower Austria, Hungary, Yug, Romania.

Hungarian glider

N. rivularis

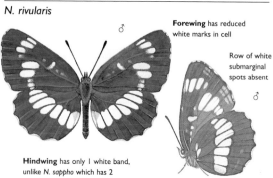

♂

Forewing has reduced white marks in cell

Row of white submarginal spots absent

♂

Hindwing has only 1 white band, unlike *N. sappho* which has 2

This species is similar in flight and distribution to the Common glider, but whereas the latter is found on shrubby hill slopes, the Hungarian glider is more restricted to woodlands and their edges. The reduced amount of white on the wings, notably the single white discal band on the hindwing, is characteristic. Although there are only two examples of this genus to be found in Europe, many more are to be found in Africa. All are blackish with white markings and have a gliding flight. *WS:* 50–54 mm; *Flight:* June–July; *Gen:* 1; *FP:* Spirea, possibly Meadowsweet (*Filipendula*); *D:* Austria, Switz, Czech, Yug, Hungary, Romania, Bulgaria, N Greece.

Camberwell beauty

Nymphalis antiopa

♂

Wide, creamy-yellow border

Row of violet-blue spots just inside margin on both wings

♂

Once known as 'Grand surprise' because of its unexpected and striking appearance, which is quite unlike that of any other European species. Originally discovered in Camberwell, but may appear anywhere

Underside dark brown, relieved by almost-white border

A regular migrant with a powerful flight, it occurs throughout Europe, although its appearance in Britain is rare. The adults feed on tree sap and bask in sun with wings outspread. *WS:* 60–65 mm; *Flight:* June–Sept; *Gen:* 1; *FP:* Willow (*Salix*); *D:* Europe.

Yellow-legged tortoiseshell

N. xanthomelas

♂

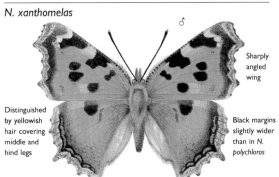

Sharply angled wing

Distinguished by yellowish hair covering middle and hind legs

Black margins slightly wider than in *N. polychloros*

This differs only slightly in pattern from the Large tortoiseshell (p 56), the most reliable diagnostic feature being its yellowish legs. It flies in damp woods. *WS:* 60–64 mm; *Flight:* July–Sept; *Gen:* 1; *FP:* Willow (*Salix*); *D:* E and SE Europe (migrates west).

55

Large tortoiseshell

Nymphalis polychloros

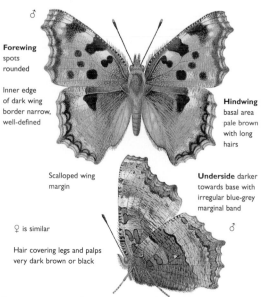

♂

Forewing spots rounded

Inner edge of dark wing border narrow, well-defined

Hindwing basal area pale brown with long hairs

Scalloped wing margin

Underside darker towards base with irregular blue-grey marginal band

♀ is similar

Hair covering legs and palps very dark brown or black

♂

Less common over its range than in former years; in Britain it is found in southern England and in parts of the Midlands. *WS:* 50–63 mm; *Flight:* June–Oct; *Gen:* 1; *FP:* Elm (*Ulmus*), Poplar (*Populus*), Willow (*Salix*); *D:* Europe (not Ireland; rare in Scand).

False comma

N. l-album   ♂

More black on wings than in *N. polychloros*

White spots near forewing apex and on costa of hindwing

Hindwing lacks any blue spots

The white costal mark on the upper hindwing distinguishes this butterfly from the similar tortoiseshell. A rare and local species, it flies mainly over lowland meadows near woods. *WS:* 60–66 mm; *Flight:* July–Sept; *Gen:* 1; *FP:* Elm (*Ulmus*); Beech (*Fagus*); *D:* Romania, Bulgaria, Hungary, Yug (migrant to Poland, S Scand).

Small tortoiseshell

Aglais urticae

Forewing has distinctive white spot near apex

Blue spots border both wings

♂

♂

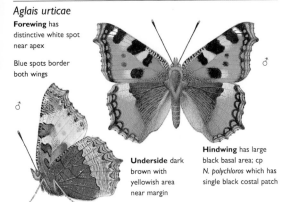

Underside dark brown with yellowish area near margin

Hindwing has large black basal area; cp *N. polychloros* which has single black costal patch

This colourful butterfly is one of the commonest in Europe. The Large tortoiseshell (p 56) is usually brighter in colour, but this may vary between specimens. The adults are common in gardens and often hibernate in houses. *WS:* 44–50 mm; *Flight:* Mar–Apr, June–Oct; *Gen:* 1–2; *FP:* Nettle (*Urtica*); *D:* Europe.
A. ichnusa from Elba, Corsica and Sardinia lacks some of the black spots on the forewing.

Comma

Polygonia c-album

♂

1st generation, f. *hutchinsoni*

Ragged wing outline is characteristic. 1st gen is brighter, less heavily marked than 2nd gen

Underside hindwing has white mark like a comma

♂

♂

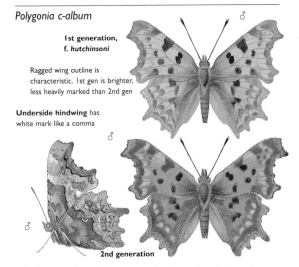

2nd generation

The lighter-coloured first generation is produced from the eggs laid by the overwintering butterflies in the spring. A rapid flyer, attracted into gardens by buddleia and Michaelmas daisies. The British population seems to be increasing, but the species is rarely abundant. *WS:* 44–48 mm; *Flight:* Mar–July; *Gen:* 2; *FP:* Nettle (*Urtica*), Hop (*Humulus*); *D:* Europe (not Scotland, N Scand).

Southern comma

Polygonia egea

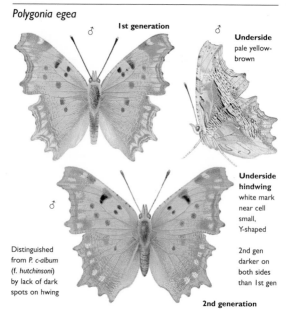

1st generation

♂

♂

Underside pale yellow-brown

Underside hindwing white mark near cell small, Y-shaped

♂

Distinguished from *P. c-album* (f. *hutchinsoni*) by lack of dark spots on hwing

2nd gen darker on both sides than 1st gen

2nd generation

This species is generally paler and less heavily marked than the Comma (p 57). It has a rapid flight, often settling on the ground, and is locally common in hot, dry valleys and on slopes up to 1400 m. The female is similar. *WS:* 44–46 mm; *Flight:* Apr–Sept; *Gen:* 2; *FP:* Pellitory of the wall (*Parietaria*); *D:* SE France, Italy, Corsica, Sardinia, Sicily, Greece, Yug.

Map butterfly

Araschnia levana

1st generation

2nd generation (f. *prorsa*)

♀

♀

Uppers yellow-brown with confused black markings

Uppers dark brown with pale yellow discal bands

As shown, the two generations are very different, although the sexes tend to be similar. The underside has an intricate linear pattern, with more purple in the margin of the first generation. Flies in light woods up to 900 m. *WS:* 32–38 mm; *Flight:* May–June, Aug–Sept; *Gen:* 2; *FP:* Nettle (*Urtica*); *D:* Denmark, C Europe (not Britain, Scand, S France, Italy, SE Balkans).

Painted lady

Vanessa cardui

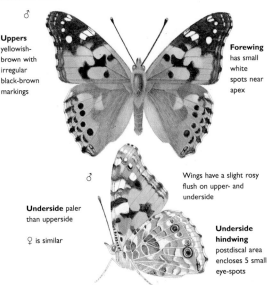

♂

Uppers
yellowish-brown with irregular black-brown markings

Forewing
has small white spots near apex

♂

Wings have a slight rosy flush on upper- and underside

Underside paler than upperside

♀ is similar

Underside hindwing postdiscal area encloses 5 small eye-spots

The Painted lady will feed on many sources of nectar and so will frequent a variety of habitats. A rapid flyer and strong migrant, it may appear and breed anywhere in Europe, but tends to be more scarce further north. The first migrants may not arrive in Britain until June. *WS:* 54–58 mm; *Flight:* Apr–Oct; *Gen:* 2–3; *FP:* Thistle (*Carduus*); *D:* Europe (as migrant from N Africa).

American painted lady

V. virginiensis   **Uppers** lack a rosy flush

Underside hwing has 2 large eye-spots in postdiscal band

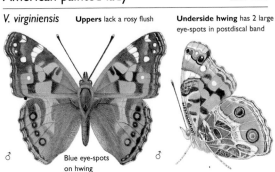

♂

Blue eye-spots on hwing

♂

Common and widespread in America, this butterfly is an occasional migrant to Europe. It is smaller than the Painted lady and is found on flowery slopes. There have been several records of its appearance in Britain, the earliest one being in 1828. *WS:* 40–50 mm; *Flight:* June–Oct; *Gen:* 1; *FP:* Cudweed (*Gnaphalium*), other Compositae; *D:* migrant to SW Europe.

59

Red admiral

Vanessa atalanta

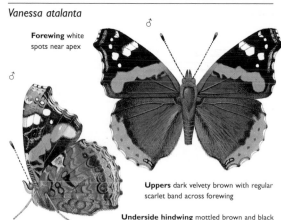

Forewing white spots near apex

Uppers dark velvety brown with regular scarlet band across forewing

Underside hindwing mottled brown and black

At rest, the Red admiral is unmistakable, with its red-and-black wings outspread. A visitor to gardens and parkland, it is attracted to a variety of flowers and, when in season, over-ripe fruit. It is a strong migrant and may appear anywhere in Europe, moving north each spring from its breeding grounds in the south. Few, if any, survive the northern winter. The butterfly is territorial in habit and may be observed patrolling the same area each day. The sexes are similar. *WS:* 56–63 mm; *Flight:* May–Oct (hibernated specimens appear early spring); *Gen:* 2–3; *FP:* Nettle (*Urtica*); *D:* Europe (rare in N Scand).

Indian red admiral

V. indica

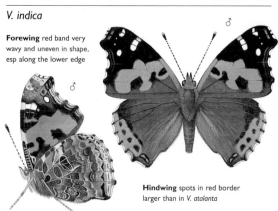

Forewing red band very wavy and uneven in shape, esp along the lower edge

Hindwing spots in red border larger than in *V. atalanta*

This does not breed in Europe, but has occured in the south as a vagrant (possibly from the Canaries). It has a powerful flight, similar to the Red admiral, and may be separated by the irregular red band on its forewing. *WS:* 54–60 mm; *Flight:* May–Oct; *Gen:* 2–3; *FP:* Nettle (*Urtica*); *D:* W Europe (incl Britain).

Peacock butterfly

Inachis io

Large 'peacock eye' on each wing is characteristic

♂

♀ is similar but slightly larger

Underside very dark, contrasting with bright upperside

This is well-camouflaged by its dark underside when at rest but, if disturbed, the eye-spots on the upperside can startle predators. The Peacock is one of the most conspicuous European butterflies, impossible to confuse with any other. Although not migratory, it is both common and widespread in many habitats. The adult over-winters. *WS:* 54–60 mm; *Flight:* July–Oct, spring; *Gen:* 1; *FP:* Nettle (*Urtica*); *D:* Europe (not N Scand, N Scot).

Pallas's fritillary

Argyronome laodice

♂

Black spots near forewing apex are smaller than the others

♂

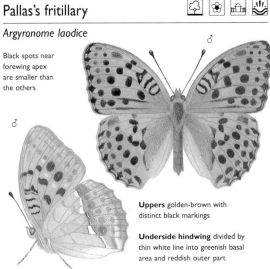

Uppers golden-brown with distinct black markings

Underside hindwing divided by thin white line into greenish basal area and reddish outer part

Female is paler with small white spot near forewing apex. Fast-flying species, found in damp woodland clearings. *WS:* 54–58 mm; *Flight:* July–Aug; *Gen:* 1; *FP:* Bog violet (*Viola palustris*); *D:* SE Finland, Poland, Hungary, Romania, Czech; migrant S Scand.

Cardinal

Argynnis pandora

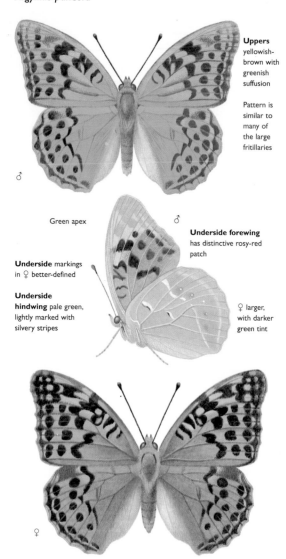

Uppers yellowish-brown with greenish suffusion

Pattern is similar to many of the large fritillaries

♂

Green apex

♂

Underside markings in ♀ better-defined

Underside forewing has distinctive rosy-red patch

Underside hindwing pale green, lightly marked with silvery stripes

♀ larger, with darker green tint

♀

The silvery bands on the underside hindwing of the Cardinal vary in different individuals and may even be absent. It has a rapid flight and is locally common in flowery meadows up to 1200 m. *WS:* 64–80 mm; *Flight:* June–July; *Gen:* 1; *FP:* Violet (*Viola*); *D:* Spain, Portugal, S France, Italy, Sicily, Corsica, Sardinia, Austria, Hungary, Czech, Balkans, Greece.

Silver-washed fritillary

A. paphia

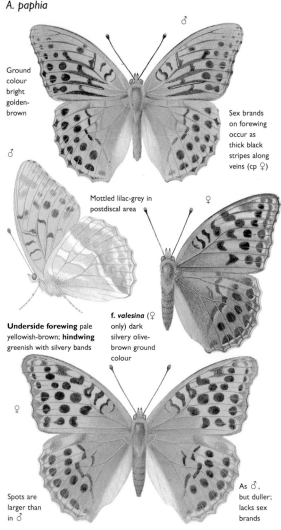

Ground colour bright golden-brown

♂

Sex brands on forewing occur as thick black stripes along veins (cp ♀)

♂

Mottled lilac-grey in postdiscal area

♀

Underside forewing pale yellowish-brown; **hindwing** greenish with silvery bands

f. valesina (♀ only) dark silvery olive-brown ground colour

♀

Spots are larger than in ♂

As ♂, but duller; lacks sex brands

This fritillary derives its name from the silvery markings on its underside. Two female forms are illustrated; the dark form, f. *valesina*, is less common and only occurs in certain localities. In Britain, the butterfly is usually found in woods, mainly in the south and southwest. The adults are partial to bramble blossom and on sunny days they may be seen descending from the trees to feed. The female lays her eggs not on the foodplant but on nearby tree trunks, where the caterpillar hibernates until spring. *WS:* 54–70 mm; *Flight:* June–Aug; *Gen:* 1; *FP:* Violet (*Viola*); *D:* Europe (not Scot, N Scand).

Dark green fritillary

Argynnis aglaja

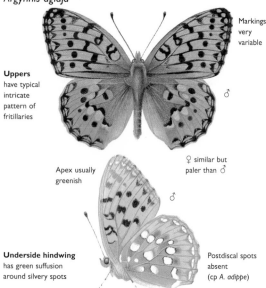

Markings very variable

Uppers
have typical intricate pattern of fritillaries

♂

Apex usually greenish

♀ similar but paler than ♂

♂

Underside hindwing
has green suffusion around silvery spots

Postdiscal spots absent
(cp *A. adippe*)

Difficult to distinguish from the High brown fritillary (p 65) without closely examining the underside of the hindwing, which in this species has silvery spots set against a greenish background. The females tend to vary more in colour on the upperside than the males, with some very pale naturally occurring forms. A rapid flyer, often found in open countryside, but also in woodlands. *WS:* 48–58 mm; *Flight:* June–July; *Gen:* 1; *FP:* Violet (*Viola*); *D:* Europe (not Corsica, Sardinia).

Corsican fritillary

A.s elisa

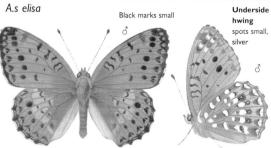

Black marks small

♂

Underside hwing
spots small, silver

♂

Although not known outside Corsica and Sardinia, it is quite widespread on these islands. The species is characterized by the small size of the spots on the uppers and the numerous small silver spots on the underside hindwing. *WS:* 46–52 mm; *Flight:* June–July; *Gen:* 1; *FP:* Violet (*Viola*); *D:* Corsica, Sardinia.

High brown fritillary

A. adippe

♂

Difficult to identify this species by its upperside pattern alone

♀

♀ broadly similar to ♂; often slightly larger and more heavily marked, with dark suffusion in basal area

♂

Underside of typical form similar in both sexes

♀

A. adippe f. cleodoxa lacks typical silver spotting on underside

Distinguished by small, reddish, silver-centred postdiscal spots on hwing

The most distinctive features of this species are on the underside hindwing, notably the row of reddish, silver-centred postdiscal spots which separate it from the Dark green fritillary (p 64). Several subspecies of the High brown fritillary have been described based on the presence or absence of silvery spots on the underside. For example, f. *cleodoxa*, a rare form in northern Europe, has pale spots without any silver (except in the postdiscal series). Recently the species has become less common in Britain and is found mainly in wooded areas of southern England. *WS:* 50–62 mm; *Flight:* June–July; *Gen:* 1; *FP:* Violet (*Viola*); *D:* Europe (not Ireland, Scot, N Scand).

Niobe fritillary

Argynnis niobe

Underside hwing spot in cell small, black-centred

Veins lined in black

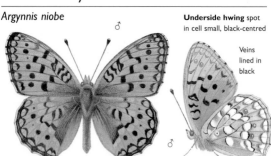

Very similar to the High brown fritillary (p 65), except that the underside hindwing is usually more greenish near the base and the silvery spots are smaller. *WS:* 46–60 mm; *Flight:* June–July; *Gen:* 1; *FP:* Violet (*Viola*); *D:* Europe (not Britain, N Scand).

Queen of Spain fritillary

Issoria lathonia

Pointed wings

Large silver spots on hwing

Sexes similar

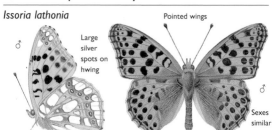

A rare migrant to Britain, its wings are more pointed than the other fritillaries and the large, silvery spots on its underside hindwing are conspicuous at rest. Common on rough, dry slopes. *WS:* 38–46 mm; *Flight:* Mar–Oct; *Gen:* 2–3 (1 in north); *FP:* Violet (*Viola*); *D:* Europe (not N Scand, Scot, Ireland).

Twin-spot fritillary

Brenthis hecate

Outer rows of black spots uniform

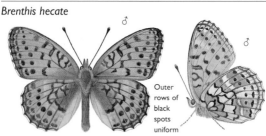

The two uniform rows of black spots running parallel to the wing edge are distinctive. Occurs in small colonies on dry slopes between 600 and 1500 m. *WS:* 36-44 mm; *Flight:* May-June; *Gen:* 1; *FP: Dorycnium; D:* Spain, S France, Italy, E Europe.

Marbled fritillary

B. daphne

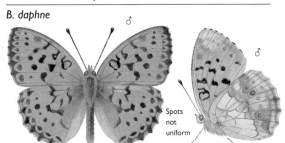

♂

Spots not uniform

♂

Distinguished from the Twin-spot fritillary (p 66) the less distinct markings on the underside hindwing and the uneven row of post-discal spots on the upper fwing. It flies in valleys up to 1200 m. Common in eastern part of range. *WS:* 42–52 mm; *Flight:* June–July; *Gen:* 1; *FP:* Bramble (*Rubus*), Violet (*Viola*), *D:* N Spain, S France, Italy, Austria, Czech, Balkans, Greece.

Lesser marbled fritillary

B. ino

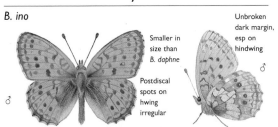

Smaller in size than *B. daphne*

Postdiscal spots on hwing irregular

Unbroken dark margin, esp on hindwing

♂

♂

A small, variable species with a rather fluttery flight. Only occurs in wet, marshy areas up to 1500 m. Many subspecies have been described. *WS:* 34–40 mm; *Flight:* June–July; *Gen:* 1; *FP:* Meadow-sweet (*Filipendula ulmaria*), Great burnet (*Sanguisorba officinalis*), *D:* Europe (not Britain, Portugal, NW France).

Bog fritillary

Boloria eunomia

♂

Underside hindwing row of black circles with white centres

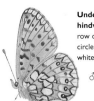

♂

The markings on the upperside are neat and regular with a zig-zag border. Life cycle unusually long: it takes 2 years to develop from egg to adult. Found in boggy areas up to 1500 m. *WS:* 40–46 mm; *Flight:* June–July; *Gen:* 1; *FP:* Bistort (*Polygonum bistorta*); *D:* Scand; local in France, Germany, Austria, Czech, Bulgaria.

Shepherd's fritillary

Boloria pales

Spots round or squarish, not elongated

Hindwing has large, dark basal area

♂

Underside forewing black marks ill-defined

♂

♀

Underside hindwing brightly marked

♀

Slightly paler ground colour than ♂

Widespread over the central and southern European mountain ranges, this butterfly rarely flies below altitudes of 1500 m. Subspecies from different localities vary in colour and pattern on the upperside; in the Pyrenees it is orange-brown with a small, dark basal area on the hindwing, while in the Apennines the subspecies is yellowish with more linear markings. *WS:* 32–40 mm; *Flight:* June–Aug; *Gen:* 1; *FP:* Violet (*Viola*); *D:* Spain, France, Italy, Austria, Switz, Poland, Germany, SE Europe.

Mountain fritillary

B. napaea

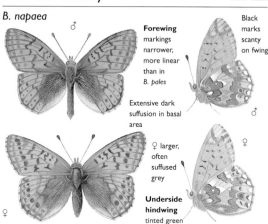

♂

Forewing markings narrower, more linear than in *B. pales*

Black marks scanty on fwing

Extensive dark suffusion in basal area

♂

♀ larger, often suffused grey

♀

Underside hindwing tinted green

♀

A true mountain species, found in small colonies usually in the wet areas at or above the tree-line from 1500 to 3000 m. The red and yellow on the underside hindwing are never as bright as in the Shepherd's fritillary. The life cycle from egg to adult usually takes 2 years. *WS:* 34–42 mm; *Flight:* July–Aug; *Gen:* 1; *FP:* Alpine bistort (*Polygonum viviparum*); *D:* France (Alps, Pyrenees), Switz, Austria, Italy (Alps), Scand (not Denmark).

Cranberry fritillary

B. aquilonaris ♂

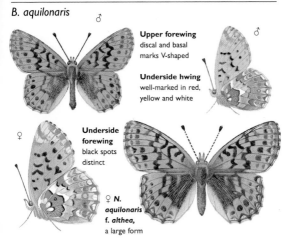

Upper forewing
discal and basal
marks V-shaped

Underside hwing
well-marked in red,
yellow and white

Underside forewing
black spots distinct

♀ **N. aquilonaris f. althea,**
a large form

This species is found in boggy areas rich in sphagnum moss where the foodplant grows, from lowlands up to 1800 m. The black markings on both sides are generally more prominent than in other *Boloria* species, although identification can still be difficult. Colonies tend to be small and isolated; specimens found in the north are often smaller than those further south. *WS:* 32–43 mm; *Flight:* June–July; *Gen:* 1; *FP:* Cranberry (*Vaccinium oxycoccus*); *D:* Scand, Poland, Czech, Austria, Germany, France, Switz.

Balkan fritillary

B. graeca ♂

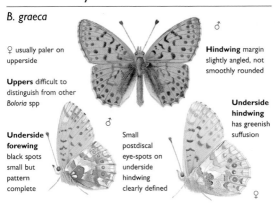

♀ usually paler on
upperside

Uppers difficult to
distinguish from other
Boloria spp

Hindwing margin
slightly angled, not
smoothly rounded

Underside hindwing
has greenish
suffusion

Underside forewing
black spots
small but
pattern
complete

Small
postdiscal
eye-spots on
underside
hindwing
clearly defined

This species is found in the Balkans and southwestern Alps. The subspecies illustrated, *B. graeca graeca*, is restricted to Greece and southern Yug, and is brighter than the more widespread subspecies, *B. graeca balcanica*. Both fly in high mountainous areas up to the tree-line at 1500 to 1800 m. *WS:* 32–40 mm; *Flight:* July; *Gen:* 1; *FP:* unknown; *D:* SE France, Bulgaria, Romania, Yug, Greece.

Pearl-bordered fritillary

Boloria euphrosyne

Uppers resemble B. selene ♂

Underside hindwing has 2 bright silver spots in addition to a border of 7 pearls.

♂

This is distinguished from the Small pearl-bordered fritillary by the pattern on the underside hindwing. A common and widespread species in woodlands and meadows up to 1800 m, although in Britain it is strangely rare in the eastern counties. The sexes are similar. *WS:* 38–46 mm; *Flight:* Apr–Aug; *Gen:* 2 (1 in north); *FP:* Violet (*Viola*); *D:* Europe (not S Spain).

Small pearl-bordered fritillary

B. selene

♂

Underside hindwing border of 7 pearls edged in black; round black spot in cell prominent

♂

The Small pearl-bordered fritillary has more black on its underside hindwing than *B. euphrosyne*, and lacks a prominent central silvery spot on this wing. The two species often fly together, but *B. selene* prefers damper areas. *WS:* 36–42 mm; *Flight:* Apr–Aug; *Gen:* 2 (1 in north); *FP:* Violet (*Viola*); *D:* Europe (not Ireland, S Spain, S Portugal, peninsular Italy, Greece, Mediterranean islands).

Titania's fritillary

B. titania

 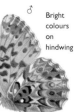

Uppers black marks heavy ♂

Bright colours on hindwing

Hindwing marginal marks on both sides strongly triangular

♂

The underside hindwing of *B. titania cypris* (illustrated) is marbled in pink, brown and yellow, although other subspecies may lack such colour contrast. *WS:* 42–48 mm; *Flight:* June–July; *Gen:* 1; *FP:* Violet (*Viola*); *D:* Alps, Balkans, Finland, Baltic states.

Arctic fritillary

B. chariclea

♂

Underside hindwing
discal band pale with
prominent silver spots

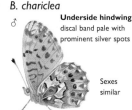

Sexes
similar

♂

The Arctic fritillary is one of the most northerly species, its capture recorded at latitude 81° 42' N. It has a circumpolar distribution and flies over dry tundra and boggy areas above 300 m. It may be confused with Frejya's frutillary where the two species fly together, but is distinguished by the pale discal band on the underside hindwing. *WS:* 32–36 mm; *Flight:* June–July; *Gen:* 1; *FP: Cassiope tetragona*, Violets; *D:* N Scand.

Frejya's fritillary

B. freija

♂

**Underside
hwing** has
prominent
black zig-zag
line in lower
discal area;
white marginal
spots large

♂

Little documentation exists on the life cycle and habits of this species. Its flight is low and slightly hesitant, and it may be found on moorland and tundra in northern Europe. *WS:* 36–44 mm; *Flight:* May––June; *Gen:* 1; *FP:* Cloudberry (*Rubus chamaemorus*), Bog whortleberry (*Vaccinium uliginosum*); *D:* Baltic states, Scand (not Denmark).

Violet fritillary

B. dia

♂

Underside hwing tinged
violet; silver spots in
discal area and on margin

Hwing sharply
angled near front
edge, not rounded
as in other *Boloria*
species

♂

A widespread species, locally common in open woodland and in hilly districts up to 1200 m. The violet-brown tinge and the dark postdiscal spots on the underside hindwing are diagnostic. The half-grown caterpillar overwinters, feeding up in the spring. *WS:* 32–34 mm; *Flight:* Apr–Oct; *Gen:* 2–3; *FP:* Violet (*Viola*), Blackberry (*Rubus*); *D:* Europe (not Britain, Scand, S Spain, S Italy).

Polar fritillary

Boloria polaris

Uppers ground colour yellowish-brown

Underside hindwing many small white marks diagnostic

♂

♂

A comparatively rare species which occurs in isolated colonies on dry, arctic tundra. The sexes are similar. *WS:* 36–38 mm; *Flight:* June–July; *Gen:* 1; *FP:* possibly Mountain avens (*Dryas octopetala*); *D:* N Scand.

Thor's fritillary

B. thore

♂

♂

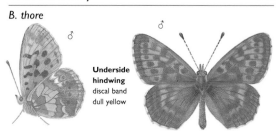

Underside hindwing discal band dull yellow

The upperside markings on Thor's fritillary are almost obscured by the dark suffusion that covers most of the wing surface. The sub-species *B. thore borealis*, which occurs in Scandinavia, has a much less dense suffusion. The species has a distinctive yellow band on the underside hwing and occurs on mountains at 900 to 2500 m. *WS:* 38–46 mm; *Flight:* June–July; *Gen:* 1; *FP:* Violet (*Viola*); *D:* Alps (Switz, Germany, Austria, Italy), Scand (not Denmark).

Frigga's fritillary

B. frigga

♀

♀

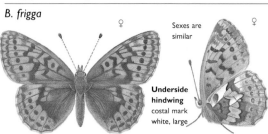

Sexes are similar

Underside hindwing costal mark white, large

This butterfly also occurs in North America where it is known as Saga's fritillary. The upperside markings are generally heavy and regular, while the underside hindwing is attractively coloured red-brown, yellow, white and lilac. Flies over damp moorlands and bogs. *WS:* 40–46 mm; *Flight:* June–July; *Gen:* 1; *FP:* Cloudberry (*Rubus chamaemorus*); *D:* N. Scand.

Dusky-winged fritillary

B. improba

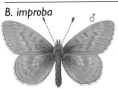

Uppers grey-brown, markings indistinct

Underside hwing pale red-brown with small white marks

A small fritillary of restricted distribution, confined to drier mountain slopes from 400 to 1200 m. The lack of clear markings on its upperside distinguishes it from the other fritillaries which have the more regular pattern. There is a narrow, white rim along the front edge of the underside hindwing, which is also a useful identification feature. *WS:* 30–34 mm; *Flight:* July–Aug; *Gen:* 1; *FP: Polygonium* species; *D:* N Scand.

Aetherie fritillary

Melitaea aetherie

Yellow and red contrast on hindwing

Marginal marks complete on upperside

Uppers ground colour orange-red

This is a North African species that occurs only very locally in southern Europe. The female is similar but often powdered grey. Prefers light woodlands and meadows at low altitudes. *WS:* 42–46 mm; *Flight:* Apr–July; *Gen:* 1; *FP:* Knapweed (*Centaurea*) species; *D:* S Spain, S Portugal, Sicily.

Freyer's fritillary

M. arduinna

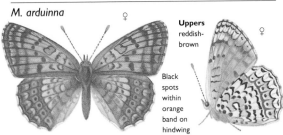

Uppers reddish-brown

Black spots within orange band on hindwing

A rare and local species in Europe, being more widespread in Asia. It resembles the Glanville fritillary (p 74), but is larger and the underside hindwing pattern differs. In Freyer's fritillary the black lunules, which line the inner border of the orange submarginal band, curve outwards. *WS:* 42–46 mm; *Flight:* May–June; *Gen:* 1; *FP:* Knapweed (*Centaurea*); *D:* SE Europe.

Knapweed fritillary

Melitaea phoebe

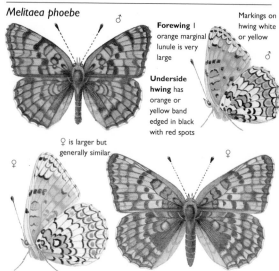

♂

Forewing l orange marginal lunule is very large

Markings on hwing white or yellow

♂

Underside hwing has orange or yellow band edged in black with red spots

♀ is larger but generally similar

♀

♀

This fritillary is very variable in size and pattern, with several described subspecies. Some specimens are lightly marked on the upperside, and have a reduced amount of black, while others are heavily patterned in black, orange and yellow. The upper hindwing has a distinct row of orange-red marks, normally without dark centres. Flies up to 2000 m over flowery slopes. *WS:* 34–50 mm; *Flight:* Apr–July; *Gen:* 2–3; *FP:* Knapweed (*Centaurea*); *D:* C and S Europe (not Britain, Scand, Belgium, Holland).

Glanville fritillary

M. cinxia

♂

Uppers with complete and regular pattern

♂

Hindwing has row of black spots in orange submarginal band

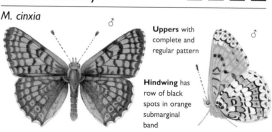

Named after Mrs Eleanor Glanville, a butterfly enthusiast of the eighteenth century (whose Will was contested on the grounds that nobody of sound mind would have such a hobby!), this species, although widespread in central Europe, is restricted to the cliffs of the Isle of Wight in Britain. The black lunules, which form the inner edge of the orange submarginal band on the underside hindwing, curve inwards, distinguishing it from the less common Freyer's fritillary (p 73). *WS:* 28–40 mm; *Flight:* May–Sept; *Gen:* 2 (1 in north); *FP:* Ribwort plantain (*Plantago lanceolata*); *D:* Europe (not S Spain, N Scand, Ireland).

M. didyma

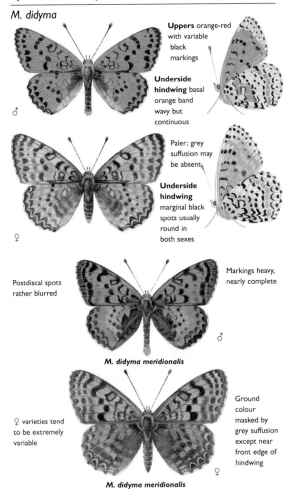

Uppers orange-red with variable black markings

Underside hindwing basal orange band wavy but continuous

♂

Paler; grey suffusion may be absent

Underside hindwing marginal black spots usually round in both sexes

♀

Postdiscal spots rather blurred

Markings heavy, nearly complete

♂

M. didyma meridionalis

♀ varieties tend to be extremely variable

Ground colour masked by grey suffusion except near front edge of hindwing

♀

M. didyma meridionalis

The Spotted fritillary is probably the most variable-patterned butterfly in Europe, with differences occurring not only between subspecies, but also between individuals from neighbouring colonies. Seasonal variation and marked sex differences can create problems of identification in the field even for the experts. The least variable features generally occur on the underside of the hind-wing, notably the round black spots in the pale yellow margin and the unbroken orange basal band. *M. didyma meridionalis* is the commonest form in southern Europe and is found in meadows and woodland clearings up to 1500 m. *WS:* 30–44 mm; *Flight:* May–Sept; *Gen:* 2–3; *FP:* Plantain (*Plantago*), Toadflax (*Linaria*); *D:* Europe (not Britain, Belgium, Holland, Scand, Corsica, Sardinia).

Lesser spotted fritillary

Melitaea trivia

♂

♀ usually larger than ♂

Underside hindwing marginal black spots triangular

♂

Similar to the Spotted fritillary (p 75), except that the marginal spots on the underside hindwing of this species tend to be triangular rather than round. It is variable in colour and pattern, with several named subspecies. Specimens of the first generation are generally larger than those of the second. *WS:* 28–38 mm; *Flight:* May–June, July–Aug; *Gen:* 2; *FP:* Great mullein (*Verbascum thapsus*); *D:* Spain, Portugal, Italy, Austria, Czech, Hungary, Romania, Yug, Bulgaria, Greece.

False heath fritillary

M. diamina

♂

Uppers dark, esp hindwing, contrasting with pale underside

Underside hwing submarginal band has row of pale spots edged in black

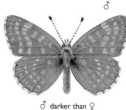

♂ darker than ♀

♂

♀

Underside hindwing marginal line yellow (♂ and ♀)

Hindwing markings pale yellow in ♀.

♀

The pattern and intensity of colour vary considerably between each specimen, so that it is very easy to mistake this species in the field for the heath fritillary (p 77) or Nickerl's fritillary (p 79). It occurs up to 2000 m and is locally common over Alpine meadows with abundant flowers. A second generation is produced in the south which will usually have a smaller wingspan than the first generation. This species overwinters in the caterpillar stage. *WS:* 32–43 mm; *Flight:* May–Aug; *Gen:* 1–2; *FP:* Cow-wheat (*Melampyrum*), Plantain (*Plantago*); *D:* Europe (not Britain, N Scand, Portugal, S Spain, Holland, W France, peninsular Italy, Greece, Mediterranean islands).

Heath fritillary

M. athalia

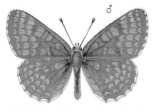

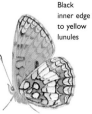

Black inner edge to yellow lunules

M. athalia athalia, a northern subspecies

M. athalia celadussa, a subspecies of SW Europe and Italy

Not as dark as those found in north

A specimen from Bihar, Hungary

Small, with bright orange ground colour

A variety found in Portugal

Larger and brighter in colour than other forms

This is one of the most widespread and variable of the fritillaries. It is usually heavily marked with black in the male but the female is often lighter. Positive identification of the Heath fritillary in the field is quite difficult, especially in continental Europe where there are many similar species which also show variation in colour, size and pattern. The most constant feature seems to be the yellowish lunules on the underside of the forewings which are edged in black. The species generally occurs in the drier areas of meadowland, but may sometimes be found in woodland clearings up to 2000 m. In Britain its appearance is restricted to a few counties in southern England. Hibernates in the caterpillar stage. *WS:* 34–46 mm; *Flight:* May–Sept; *Gen:* 1–2; *FP:* Cow-wheat (*Melampyrum*), Plantain (*Plantago*); *D:* Europe (not Ireland, Scot, Corsica, Sardinia).

Provençal fritillary

Melitaea deione

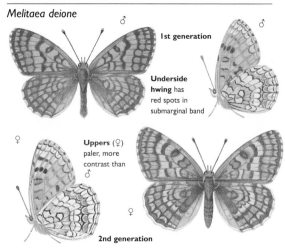

♂

1st generation

Underside hwing has red spots in submarginal band

Uppers (♀) paler, more contrast than ♂

♀

♂

♀

2nd generation

Easily confused with the Heath fritillary (p 77); usually the Provençal fritillary is a paler orange-brown with thinner black markings. One feature that is not always constant (shown in the male specimen above) is a dumb-bell-shaped black mark near the hind margin of the upper forewing. Flies over mountain slopes. *WS:* 32–46 mm; *Flight:* May–Sept; *Gen:* 2; *FP:* Toadflax (*Linaria*) and others; *D:* Spain, Portugal, S France, Alps.

Meadow fritillary

M. parthenoides

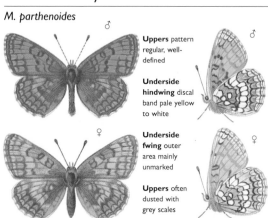

♂

Uppers pattern regular, well-defined

Underside hindwing discal band pale yellow to white

Underside fwing outer area mainly unmarked

♂

♀

♀

Uppers often dusted with grey scales

This flies close to the ground over hill slopes up to 2000 m. At low altitudes there are two generations, but higher up the species is single-brooded, with dark forms sometimes occurring. *WS:* 30–36 mm; *Flight:* May–Sept; *Gen:* 1–2; *FP:* Toadflax (*Linaria*); *D:* Spain, Portugal, France, S Germany, Switz, N Italy (Alps).

Grisons fritillary

M. varia

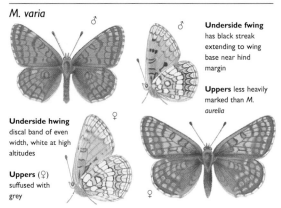

Underside fwing has black streak extending to wing base near hind margin

Uppers less heavily marked than *M. aurelia*

Underside hwing discal band of even width, white at high altitudes

Uppers (♀) suffused with grey

Grisons fritillary is found mainly in low vegetation on mountain slopes from 1000 to 2000 m. A very difficult species to identify in the field; Nickerl's fritillary, which is similar and flies in the same area, tends to have broader wings and more complete markings. *WS:* 30–38 mm; *Flight:* June–Aug; *Gen:* 1; *FP:* Gentian (*Gentiana*); *D:* SE France, Switz, Austria, Italy (Alps, Apennines).

Nickerl's fritillary

M. aurelia

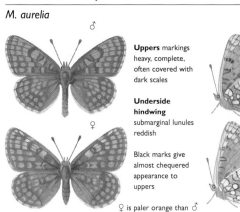

Uppers markings heavy, complete, often covered with dark scales

Underside hindwing submarginal lunules reddish

Black marks give almost chequered appearance to uppers

♀ is paler orange than ♂

Widely distributed in eastern and central Europe, this rather small dark species can be just as troublesome as the other fritillaries to name correctly. It usually flies in the wetter areas of moorlands up to 1500 m, and over bogs and damp meadows. The species overwinters as a caterpillar, feeding up in the spring before pupating. Occasionally two generations are produced in the south. *WS:* 28–32 mm; *Flight:* June–July; *Gen:* 1–2; *FP:* Plantain (*Plantago*), Speedwell (*Veronica*), Cow-wheat (*Melampyrum*); *D:* N and E France, Germany, Belgium, Switz, Czech, Austria, N Italy, Hungary, Balkans.

Assmann's fritillary

Melitaea britomartis

♂

Uppers like *M. aurelia*, but slightly darker

Underside hwing orange submarginal lunules have dark inner edge

♂

Mainly found in eastern Europe, although it does occur locally in north Italy. May be seen on the wing with Nickerl's fritillary (p 79), which is usually smaller, but the two species are not easy to distinguish. The second generation (south only) is smaller than the first. *WS:* 30–36 mm; *Flight:* May–Aug; *Gen:* 2; *FP:* Plantain (*Plantago*), Speedwell (*Veronica*); *D:* S Sweden, Poland, Germany, Romania, Hungary, Bulgaria, Czech, Italy.

Little fritillary

M. asteria

♂

Uppers very dark in basal area

Underside hwing has single black marginal line

A very small, dark fritillary, restricted to the eastern Alps. Flies over grassy slopes at altitudes above 2000 m. The female is usually paler than the male. *WS:* 28–30 mm; *Flight:* May–Aug; *Gen:* 1; *FP:* unknown; *D:* Alps (Switz, N Italy, Austria).

Scarce fritillary

Euphyhydras maturna

♂

Underside fwing yellowish lunules along margin are uneven in size

Uppers reddish with wide red bands on hwing, bordered internally by row of cream spots

♂

A species of scattered distribution, with isolated populations occurring in wooded valleys, often near streams. It is a rapid flyer and lays its eggs on trees, where the caterpillars then overwinter in colonies beneath a silken web. In spring they disperse and feed on low plants before pupating. *WS:* 42–50 mm; *Flight:* May–July; *Gen:* 1; *FP:* Ash (*Fraxinus*), Poplar (*Populus*), Plantain (*Plantago*); *D:* N France, S Scand, Germany, Poland, Austria, Hungary, Romania, Yug, Bulgaria, NW Greece.

Asian fritillary

E. wolfensbergeri

♂

Ground colour orange-red.
♀ larger, paler, resembles
♀ E. cynthia (except for thin
line on underside hindwing)

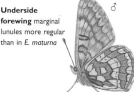

♂

**Underside
forewing** marginal
lunules more regular
than in *E. maturna*

Upper hindwing has
broad dark margin

Underside hindwing central
yellow band encloses thin black line

Risk of confusing this species with the Scarce fritillary (p 80) is unlikely as geographically their ranges do not overlap, and the Asian fritillary flies at higher altitudes, usually above 1000 m. Confusion is more likely between the females of this species and Cynthia's fritillary (below); the latter lacks a thin black line in the yellow band on the underside hindwing. *WS:* 38–42 mm; *Flight;* June–July; *Gen:* 1; *FP; Lonicera Caerulea; D:* Alps.

Cynthia's fritillary

E. cynthia

♂

Uppers white
ground colour
characteristic

♂

Hindwing (both
sides) often has
row of small black
spots in red band,
but shown only in
♀ specimen here

**Underside
hindwing**
yellow band
near centre
unmarked

♀

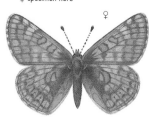

♀

Chiefly an Alpine species, although it also occurs in the mountains of Bulgaria. Specimens may be found on sparsely covered slopes as high as 3000 m, but these tend to be smaller and darker than those which fly lower down. The caterpillars are gregarious and overwinter in a web. *WS:* 32–42 mm; *Flight:* May–Aug; *Gen:* 1; *FP:* Lady's mantle (*Alchemilla*), Plantain (*Plantago*); *D:* Germany, Austria, S France, N Italy, Bulgaria, Macedonia.

Lapland fritillary

Euphydryas iduna

Uppers creamy white with reddish bands and greyish-black markings

Underside not as dusky as topside

Small colonies of the Lapland fritillary are quite common in the far north of Europe, usually in areas with few trees. Always a local species, it is generally found in moorland bogs and on mountainsides up to 800 m. The sexes are similar. *WS:* 36–38 mm; *Flight:* June–July; *Gen:* 1; *FP:* Plantain (*Plantago*), Speedwell (*Veronica*); *D:* N Norway, N Sweden, N Finland.

Spanish fritillary

E. desfontainii

Underside paler than uppers

Underside fwing has prominent black spots near middle (cp *E. aurinia*)

E. desfontainii baetica

Forewing marginal marks dark, triangular, enclosing yellow lunules

Hindwing orange postdiscal band contains black spots visible on underside (both sexes)

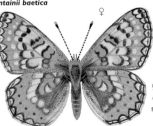

Forewing yellow spots in orange-red postdiscal band

♀ larger than ♂, but with similar pattern

E. desfontainii baetica

This species and the Marsh fritillary (p 83) differ from the preceding fritillaries because they always have fairly conspicuous black spots contained within the orange-red postdiscal band on the hindwing. The two species may be separated by the black markings on the underside forewing, which are more prominent in the Spanish fritillary. The European subspecies, which is illustrated above, is paler red than the nominate subspecies, *E. desfontainii desfontainii*, which occurs in North Africa. In Europe the colonies are widely separated and often show variation in colour and pattern. The adults fly in hilly areas between 600 and 1200 m. *WS:* 40–48 mm; *Flight:* May–June; *Gen:* 1; *FP:* Knapweed (*Centaurea*); *D:* S and E Spain (up to Pyrenees).

Marsh fritillary

E. aurinia

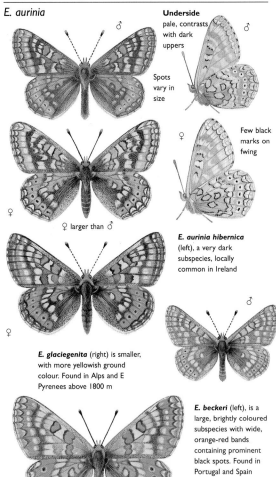

Underside
pale, contrasts
with dark
uppers

♂

Spots
vary in
size

♂

Few black
marks on
fwing

♀

♀ larger than ♂

E. aurinia hibernica
(left), a very dark
subspecies, locally
common in Ireland

♀

E. glaciegenita (right) is smaller,
with more yellowish ground
colour. Found in Alps and E
Pyrenees above 1800 m

♂

E. beckeri (left), is a
large, brightly coloured
subspecies with wide,
orange-red bands
containing prominent
black spots. Found in
Portugal and Spain

♀

A variable species with differences occurring between individuals
of neighbouring colonies, but generally the species is easy to
recognize. As well as having a liking for wet, boggy areas, the
Marsh fritillary also flies over dry mountain slopes up to 1500 m.
Common in west Britain, with a few isolated populations occurring in west Scotland. The caterpillars live gregariously under a
silken web, and hibernate in this form. Very similar related species
E. beckeri, *E. glaciegenita* and *E. provincialis* occur locally in Europe.
WS: 30–46 mm; *Flight:* May–June; *Gen:* 1; *FP:* Plantain (*Plantago*), Devilsbit scabious (*Succisa pratensis*); *D:* Europe (not Norway
or Mediterranean islands; rare in peninsular Italy).

Brown butterflies Satyridae

Although most species in this family are a shade of brown, there are exceptions, notably the Marbled white (p 85) which at first looks more like a Pierid. Generally they are medium-sized, darkly coloured butterflies with intricately patterned wings, incorporating black-and-white ringed eye-spots. One feature of the forewing peculiar to the Browns is the veins, which are swollen at the base. The caterpillars taper at both ends, and often have fork-shaped tails.

Sandy-coloured body, covered in down, with several dark longitudinal stripes

Grayling caterpillar

Active by day and night

Esper's marbled white

Melanargia russiae ♂

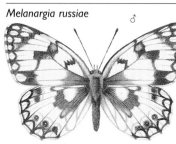

Forewing black mark across cell usually a narrow zig-zag

Hindwing large white spot in dark basal area; 2 or 3 eye-spots visible

Uppers delicate black markings on white background

♂

♀ has darker, more extensive black markings and is usually more yellowish

Ground colour varies from white to yellow

Underside hindwing pale grey markings strongly outlined in black; eye-spots very distinct

Esper's marbled white is less common and much more delicately marked than the Marbled white (p 85). Several subspecies have been described based on differences in size and pattern; the subspecies *M. russiae japygia*, which is found very locally in the Apennines of southern Italy and in Sicily, is slightly smaller and more heavily marked with black than the specimen shown above (from western Europe). The species occurs in widely scattered colonies on dry, stony mountainous slopes between 1000 and 2000 m. *WS:* 50–60 mm; *Flight:* July; *Gen:* 1; *FP:* Annual meadow grass (*Poa annua*); *D:* Spain, Portugal, S and C France, Italy (Apennines), Sicily, Albania, Balkans.

Marbled white

M. galathea

Forewing central cell lacks any narrow black cross-bars

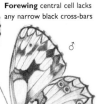

Uppers have distinctive black-and-white chequered pattern; extent of black may vary in both sexes

Underside hindwing submarginal band enclosing eye-spots broken in middle; eye-spots not always visible on uppers

♀ usually larger than ♂

Underside hindwing tinted ochre-yellow in ♀; dark discal band very narrow near top of cell (♂ and ♀)

This is widespread in grassy areas up to 1800 m. The female lays her eggs in flight and they fall at random. Found in Britain mainly in southern and central areas, especially chalk downs. Slow flyer, often settling with wings outspread. *WS:* 46–56 mm; *Flight:* June–Aug; *Gen:* 1; *FP:* grasses; *D:* Europe (not Scand, Ireland).

Southern marbled white

M. lachesis

Black markings on upperside reduced compared with *M. galathea*.

Hindwing with little black in discal cell

Slightly larger than the Marbled white, it has less black in median and basal areas on upperside of wings. *WS:* 50–57 mm; *Flight:* June–Aug; *Gen:* 1; *FP:* grasses; *D:* Spain, Portugal, SE France.

Balkan marbled white

Melanargia larissa

♂

Forewing cell crossed by narrow black line

Variable amount of black on wings; at times may obscure cell-bar in forewing

♂

Uppers basal area of both wings extensively suffused with black

Underside hindwing eye-spots distinct; basal area pale grey

Generally confined to the dry slopes of southeastern Europe, although several subspecies are known to occur in Asia. The females are usually larger with more yellowish undersides. The subspecies *M. larissa herta* is recognized by the greater amount of white on its wings, although there is still a dark suffusion over the basal area. *WS:* 50–60 mm; *Flight:* June–July; *Gen:* 1; *FP:* grasses; *D:* Bulgaria, Greece, Yug, Albania.

Western marbled white

M. occitanica

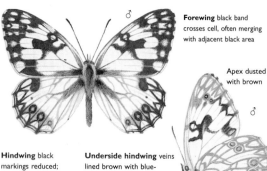

♂

Forewing black band crosses cell, often merging with adjacent black area

Apex dusted with brown

♂

Hindwing black markings reduced; eye-spots visible from underneath

Underside hindwing veins lined brown with blue-centred eye-spots (absent in form that occurs in Sicily)

Distinguished from other marbled whites by the brown veins on the underside hindwing; the patterning also tends to be lighter. Isolated colonies on dry hill slopes up to 1800 m in southern Europe. Females are often bigger with more brown suffusion on the underside. *WS:* 46–56 mm; *Flight:* May–July; *Gen:* 1; *FP:* grasses; *D:* Spain, Portugal, S France, NW Italy (coast), Corsica. **Sicilian marbled white, *Melanargia phenrua*** has reduced black on upperside compared with *M. occitanica*. *WS:* 50–54 mm; *Flight:* May–June; *Gen:* 1; *FP:* grasses; *D:* Sicily.

Italian marbled white

M. arge

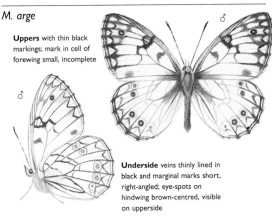

Uppers with thin black markings; mark in cell of forewing small, incomplete

♂

♂

Underside veins thinly lined in black and marginal marks short, right-angled; eye-spots on hindwing brown-centred, visible on upperside

The Italian marbled white is the most delicately marked of its kind, similar in pattern to *M. occitanica* (p 86) but with much less black on its wings. Isolated populations may be found throughout the mountainous areas of peninsular Italy and Sicily, from quite low altitudes to over 2000 m. Should not be mistaken in the field for *M. ines* (below) as geographically their ranges are completely separate. The sexes are similar. *WS:* 50–56 mm; *Flight:* May–June; *Gen:* 1; *FP:* unknown, probably grasses; *D:* Italy, Sicily.

Spanish marbled white

M. ines

♂ **Forewing** black bar across cell well-defined

Striations along costa of underside fwing and hwing

♂

Underside hindwing eye-spots prominent, black-ringed with blue pupils; marginal marks more rounded than in *M. arge* and *M. occitanica*

A widespread species of North Africa but in Europe its range is restricted to Spain and Portugal, where it may be quite common in southern and central regions. It flies over grassy mountain slopes up to 2000 m, the specimens from higher altitudes being on the wing much later in the year. Two blue-pupilled eye-spots are normally conspicuous on both sides of the forewing, in addition to those that are plainly visible on the hindwing. The female is larger and yellower than the male. *WS:* 46–50 mm; *Flight:* Apr–June; *Gen:* 1; *FP: Brachypodium; D:* Spain, Portugal.

Woodland grayling

Hipparchia fagi

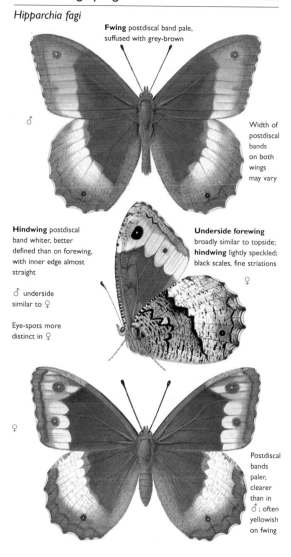

Fwing postdiscal band pale, suffused with grey-brown

♂

Width of postdiscal bands on both wings may vary

Hindwing postdiscal band whiter, better defined than on forewing, with inner edge almost straight

♂ underside similar to ♀

Eye-spots more distinct in ♀

Underside forewing broadly similar to topside; **hindwing** lightly speckled; black scales, fine striations

♀

♀

Postdiscal bands paler, clearer than in ♂; often yellowish on fwing

A few species of the genus Hipparchia, virtually indistinguishable in the field, are not included here. Size is often the most reliable guide, the Woodland grayling invariably being the largest. Also, habitat preferences are different, the present species flying in open woods at low altitudes (rarely above 1200 m), frequently settling on trunks with its wings closed. *WS:* 66–76 mm; *Flight:* July–Aug; *Gen:* 1; *FP:* grasses, esp *Holcus*; *D:* S and C Europe (not Britain, Scand, NW France, C and S Spain, Portugal, Germany).

88

Rock grayling

H. hermione

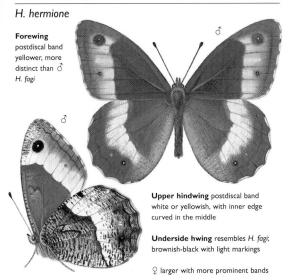

Forewing postdiscal band yellower, more distinct than ♂ *H. fagi*

♂

♂

Upper hindwing postdiscal band white or yellowish, with inner edge curved in the middle

Underside hwing resembles *H. fagi*; brownish-black with light markings

♀ larger with more prominent bands

Smaller in size and more widespread than the Woodland grayling (p 88), this species flies in mountainous areas up to 1800 m in the south, but further north it is found at lower levels. *WS:* 56–66 mm; *Flight:* June–July; *Gen:* 1; *FP:* grasses, esp *Brachypodium*; *D:* Spain, Portugal, France, Germany, Austria, Czech, Poland, SE Norway (rare in C Italy).
H. syriaca (Eastern rock grayling) formerly a subspecies of *H. hermione,* cannot be separated from this or *H. fagi* by external features alone. *WS:* 62-66 mm; *D:* Yug, Greece.

Corsican grayling

H. neomiris ♂

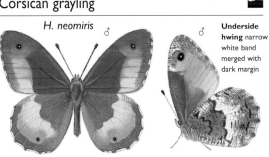

♂

Underside hwing narrow white band merged with dark margin

Uppers dark brown with wide orange-yellow bands

♀ lighter brown, with less clouding on forewing apex

This species has only been recorded from a few Mediterranean islands, where it flies mainly in dry mountainous areas between 900 and 2000 m. In Elba it occurs at lower altitudes. *WS:* 46–50 mm; *Flight:* June–July; *Gen:* 1; *FP:* unknown, probably grasses; *D:* Corsica, Sardinia, Elba.

Grayling

Hipparchia semele

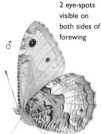

♂

2 eye-spots visible on both sides of forewing

♂

Fwing yellow postdiscal band poorly defined, suffused with brown in ♂, but more distinct and less dusky in ♀

♀ larger than ♂, with bigger eye-spots

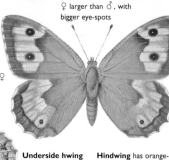

♀

♀

Underside hwing marbled light and dark grey, darkest in basal area

Hindwing has orange-yellow band crossed by dark veins and enclosing 1 small eye-spot

A complex species with many subspecies: there are several in Britain alone. For example, *H. semele thyone* from North Wales emerges earlier than the typical form and is small and subdued in colour, while subsp *atlantica* from the Inner Hebrides is brightly marked. Tends to prefer sandy coastal areas and is difficult to spot when its wings are closed. *WS:* 42–50 mm; *Flight:* May–Aug; *Gen:* 1; *FP:* grasses, esp *Festuca*; *D:* Europe (not N Scand).

Cretan grayling

H. cretica

♂

Rather dusky, like *H. semele.* ♀ brighter

♂

Confined to Crete (where the Grayling does not occur). *WS:* 52–60 mm; *Flight:* May-June; *Gen:* 1; *FP:* unknown; *D:* Crete.

Southern grayling

H. aristaeus

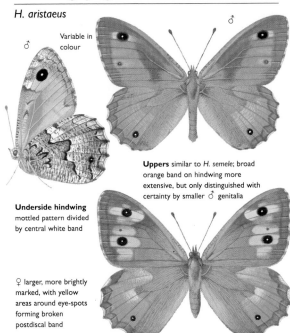

Variable in colour ♂

♂

Uppers similar to *H. semele*; broad orange band on hindwing more extensive, but only distinguished with certainty by smaller ♂ genitalia

Underside hindwing mottled pattern divided by central white band

♀ larger, more brightly marked, with yellow areas around eye-spots forming broken postdiscal band

This species has a large amount of orange on its wings; found on rough ground. *WS:* 50–54 mm; *Flight:* June–Aug; *Gen:* 1; *FP:* grasses; *D:* Corsica, Sardinia, Sicily, S Italy, Greece. A complex of several closely allied species that are difficult to distinguish, including *H. ballettoi*, *H. blachieri*, *H. volgensis*, *H. maderensis* and *H. senthes*.

Tree grayling

H. statilinus

Uppers dark grey-brown with indistinct markings

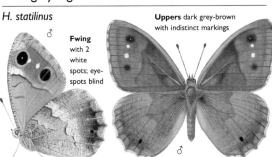

♂

Fwing with 2 white spots; eye-spots blind

♂

Found in sparse woodland. Variable; the eye-spots of female usually have white centres. *WS:* 44–46 mm; *Flight:* July–Sept; *Gen:* 1; *FP:* grasses, esp *Bromus*; *D:* C and S Europe (not Britain, Scand). *H. fatua* (Freyer's grayling) is larger; markings more distinct. *WS:* 60–68 mm; *Flight:* July–Aug; *D:* Yug, Bulgaria, Greece.

Striped grayling

Hipparchia fidia

♂

Uppers dark grey-brown with obscure markings; 2 white spots between eyespots larger in ♀

Eye-spots obscure

Hindwing margin scalloped; thin black submarginal line just visible

♂

♀ larger, markings better defined on topside, often with few small white spots on hindwing

Underside hindwing whitish grey and brown with conspicuous dark zig-zag lines

Pattern on underside is diagnostic

The upperside resembles the Tree grayling (p 91) in colour and markings, the species being distinguished by the zig-zag pattern on the underside hindwing. Occurs in small local colonies on sparsely covered rocky slopes up to 2000 m. *WS:* 56–62 mm; *Flight:* July–Aug; *Gen:* 1; *FP:* grasses, esp *Oryzopsis*; *D:* Spain, Portugal, S France, N Italy.

Nevada grayling

Pseudochazara hippolyte

♂

♀ usually larger, with slightly darker basal area

Pale yellow band with well-defined edges stretches across both wings

Underside like *H. semele*, but paler, more yellowish

Flies over mountain slopes between 2000 and 3000 m. Very local in western Europe, known only from the Sierra Nevada. *WS:* 50–52 mm; *Flight:* June–July; *FP:* unknown; *D:* Spain.
P. graeca (Grecian grayling) has a darker yellow postdiscal band, and lacks any white marks between its 2 black eye-spots (separating it from *P. amymone* and *P. cingovskii*, p 94). Occurs on mountains, *WS:* 50–52 mm; *Flight:* July–Aug; *D:* Greece.

Hermit

Chazara briseis

♂

Forewing front margin pale yellow or whitish

Uppers dark brown with creamy white postdiscal band on both wings, divided by dark veins on forewing (not hindwing)

♀

Eye-spots in ♀ often have white centres

♀ larger, postdiscal band on forewing more uneven than in ♂

Underside hindwing has mottled grey-brown pattern, markings obscure

The size of this butterfly is very variable, with a wingspan difference of as much as 26 mm between a small male specimen and a large female. Locally common on dry stony slopes from lowlands to 2500 m. *WS:* 42–68 mm; *Flight:* May–Aug; *Gen:* 1; *FP:* grasses, esp Blue moor grass (*Sesleria caerulea*); *D:* C and S Europe (not Britain, N France, Scand, Corsica, Sardinia).

Southern hermit

C. prieuri

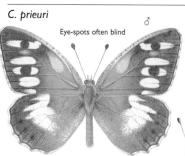

♂

Eye-spots often blind

Underside hwing strongly patterned, with dark V-shaped submarginal marks

♂

Separated from *C. briseis* by buff streak in forewing cell (♂ only) and more broken appearance of white postdiscal band

The female is usually larger with less distinct markings on the underside hindwing. This species has a more restricted range than the Hermit and flies over mountainous terrain above 900 m. *WS:* 54–66 mm; *Flight:* June–July; *Gen:* 1; *FP:* unknown; *D:* Spain.

White-banded grayling

Pseudochazara anthelea

♂

Fwing has conspicuous black sex brand in cell (♂ only); eye-spots large, may lack white centres

White band prominent on forewing, but short with tawny suffusion on hindwing

♀ similar but larger

This flies over rough ground from lowlands to 1600 m. *WS:* 46–50 mm; *Flight:* June–July; *Gen:* 1; *FP:* unknown; *D:* Greece, SE Yug, Albania, Bulgaria, Crete.

Brown's grayling

P. amymone

♂

Eye-spots usually lack white centres

♂

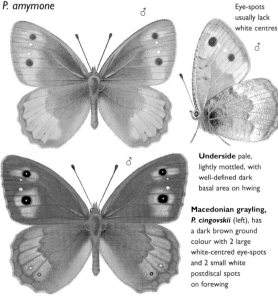

♂

Underside pale, lightly mottled, with well-defined dark basal area on hwing

Macedonian grayling, P. cingovskii (left), has a dark brown ground colour with 2 large white-centred eye-spots and 2 small white postdiscal spots on forewing

Brown's grayling has two barely discernible white spots enclosed within the pale orange-yellow band on the forewing. This band is very wide where it extends across the hindwing and usually lacks dark cross-veins. Found on rough ground at low altitudes. *WS:* 52–54 mm; *Flight:* July–Aug; *Gen:* 1; *FP:* unknown; *D:* NW Greece. **Macedonian grayling, P. cingovskii** flies in more mountainous areas above 1000 m. The wing bands are more orange in colour; with dark venation and two small, white-centred eye-spots on the hindwing. Related species *P. orestes*, found in roughly the same area. *WS:* 50–54 mm; *Flight:* July; *FP:* unknown; *D:* Yug, NW Greece.

Grey Asian grayling

P. geyeri

♀

Markings less clear in ♂

Arrow-marks near margin of hwing

♀

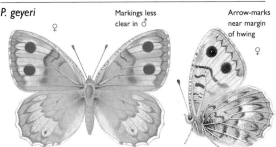

A yellowish-grey species that occurs locally on dry rocky slopes up to 2000 m (more widespread in Asia). *WS:* 48–50 mm; *Flight:* July–Aug; *Gen:* 1; *FP:* unknown; *D:* SE Yug, Albania.

Norse grayling

Oeneis norna ♂

♂

More than 2 eye-spots may occur

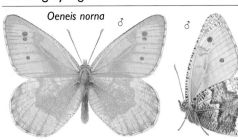

This grayling has a dark central band edged with white on its underside hindwing. It flies over bogs from 900 m down to the northern coast. The female is paler with white-centred eye-spots. *WS:* 53–56 mm; *Flight:* July; *Gen:* 1; *FP:* grasses; *D:* N Scand.

Arctic grayling

O. bore

Uppers pale grey-brown with indistinct pattern

♂

Eye-spots absent

♂

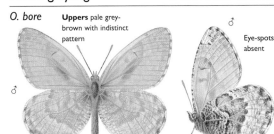

Often rather worn in appearance, this species is active only in sunshine, and is found in sandy coastal and mountainous areas. The female is similar but with a yellow flush on upper forewing. Lives for 2 years as a caterpillar. *WS:* 44–50 mm; *Flight:* July; *Gen:* 1; *FP:* grasses, esp Sheep's fescue (*Festuca ovina*); *D:* N Scand.

Alpine grayling

Oeneis glacialis

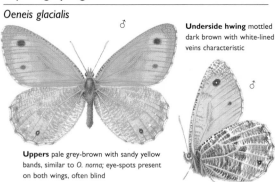

♂

Underside hwing mottled dark brown with white-lined veins characteristic

♂

Uppers pale grey-brown with sandy yellow bands, similar to *O. norna*; eye-spots present on both wings, often blind

Flies at high altitudes (above 2000 m) over grassy Alpine slopes. Abundant only every other year in some localities, presumably because the caterpillar takes 2 years to grow to full size. *WS:* 50–56 mm; *Flight:* June–Aug; *Gen:* 1; *FP:* grasses, esp Sheep's feacue (*Festuca ovina*); *D:* Alps (Italy, Switz, Austria, Bavaria).

Baltic grayling

O. jutta

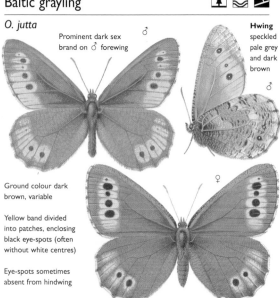

Prominent dark sex brand on ♂ forewing

♂

Hwing speckled pale grey and dark brown

♂

Ground colour dark brown, variable

Yellow band divided into patches, enclosing black eye-spots (often without white centres)

Eye-spots sometimes absent from hindwing

♀

The female is often noticeably larger than the male with bigger and more constant eye-spots. Strictly a lowland species, it may be common in boggy areas with sparse conifer vegetation. The male frequently settles on tree trunks, while the female keeps closer to the ground. The caterpillar probably takes 2 years to become fully grown. *WS:* 54–56 mm; *Flight:* May–July; *Gen:* 1; *FP:* grasses; *D:* Scand, Poland, E Germany, Baltic states.

Black satyr

Satyrus actaea

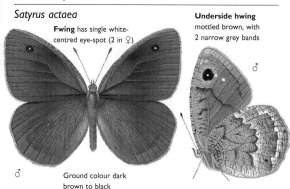

Fwing has single white-centred eye-spot (2 in ♀)

Underside hwing
mottled brown, with
2 narrow grey bands

♂

♂

Ground colour dark
brown to black

A variable species with many local races; in some specimens the eye-spot is very large and a few males may even have an additional spot on the forewing. The females are larger and paler, with two eye-spots ringed in yellow, and an underside forewing which is predominantly brown. It is found on dry mountain slopes above 1000 m. *WS:* 48–56 mm; *Flight:* July–Aug; *Gen* 1; *FP:* grasses, esp *Bromus*; *D:* Spain, Portugal, S France, N Italy.

Great sooty satyr

S. ferula

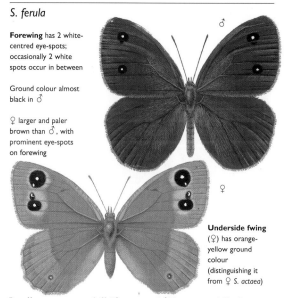

Forewing has 2 white-centred eye-spots;
occasionally 2 white spots occur in between

Ground colour almost
black in ♂

♀ larger and paler
brown than ♂, with
prominent eye-spots
on forewing

♂

♀

Underside fwing
(♀) has orange-yellow ground
colour
(distinguishing it
from ♀ *S. actaea*)

Locally common on hillsides up to 1600 m, especially in stony, sparsely vegetated areas. *WS:* 50–60 mm; *Flight:* July–Aug; *Gen:* 1; *FP:* grasses, esp *Deschampsia caespitosa*; *D:* S France, N Spain, Italy, Switz, Austria, Yug, Bulgaria, Greece.

Dryad

Minois dryas

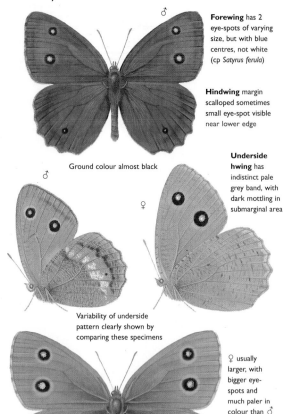

Forewing has 2 eye-spots of varying size, but with blue centres, not white (cp *Satyrus ferula*)

Hindwing margin scalloped sometimes small eye-spot visible near lower edge

Ground colour almost black

Underside hwing has indistinct pale grey band, with dark mottling in submarginal area

Variability of underside pattern clearly shown by comparing these specimens

♀ usually larger, with bigger eye-spots and much paler in colour than ♂

Hindwing scalloping on margin often more pronounced in ♀

The Dryad has a wider distribution in central Europe than the previous two satyr butterflies, with local colonies scattered throughout most of its range, but sometimes absent from large areas. It has a slow, rather fluttery flight, usually just above the ground, and visits dry shrubland, woodland clearings and grassy slopes up to 1500 m in the Alps. Both sexes vary in pattern and intensity of colour but are distinguishable from the Great sooty satyr (p 97) by the blue-pupilled eye-spots on the forewing and the scalloped edge of the hindwing. The species overwinters as a caterpillar and pupates in the spring. *WS:* 54–70 mm; *Flight:* June–Sept; *Gen:* 1 (2 in south?); *FP:* grasses; *D:* N Spain, Germany, France, Switz, N Italy, Austria, Yug, Bulgaria, Romania.

Great banded grayling

Kanetisa circe

Forewing has blind eye-spot near apex

♂

Ground colour dark brown to black

Broad white band crossed by veins on both wings

♀ similar but larger

An active flyer found in lightly wooded areas up to 1500 m; if disturbed it usually flies well out of reach before settling again, often on tree trunks. The underside pattern is similar but mottled. *WS:* 66–80 mm; *Flight:* June–Aug; *Gen:* 1; *FP:* grasses, including *Bromus*; *D:* C and S Europe (not Britain, Scand, Holland).

Arran brown

Erebia ligea

Eye-spots usually with white pupils

♂

Uppers dark brown with wide red bands, enclosing 3 or 4 eye-spots on forewing and 3 on hindwing

♂

Chequered wing fringes (♂ and ♀)

Underside hwing has variable white streak extending from costa (more conspicuous in ♀)

♀ paler, with bands more orange in colour

♀

This is found in meadows near forests, especially in mountainous areas, but further north it prefers lowlands. Reports from Arran in Scotland need confirming. Spends 2 years as a caterpillar. *WS:* 48–54 mm; *Flight:* June–Aug; *Gen:* 1; *FP:* grasses, esp *Milium*; *D:* Scand, C France, Germany, Italy, Alps, Carpathians, Balkans.

False grayling

Arethusana arethusa ♂

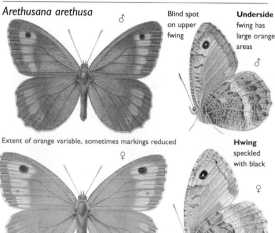

Blind spot on upper fwing

Underside fwing has large orange areas ♂

Extent of orange variable, sometimes markings reduced ♀

Hwing speckled with black ♀

♀ larger, paler, with wider orange bands ♀

Underside hwing white central band obscure

Orange spots pointed towards margin

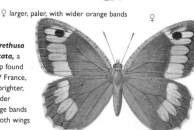

A. arethusa dentata, a subsp found in W France, has brighter, broader orange bands on both wings

Underside more strongly patterned and brightly coloured than typical form ♀

♂ is similar but orange bands on upperside not so sharply defined at edges

Underside hwing veins lined in grey

The amount of orange on the upperside is extremely variable; some subspecies, such as the one above, have wide bands of brilliant orange-yellow, while others, such as *A. arethusa boabdil* from Andalusia in Spain, have very indistinct markings. The latter has white veins and a conspicuous white central band on its underside hindwing. Widespread but always local, this species flies over heathlands up to 1500 m, especially in limestone areas. The pupa lies on the soil surface. *WS:* 44–48 mm; *Flight:* July–Aug; *Gen:* 1; *FP:* grasses, esp *Festuca*; *D:* Spain, Portugal, France, Switz, N Italy, C Germany, Balkans, Greece, E Europe.

Large ringlet

Erebia euryale

♂

Black eye-spots sometimes have white centres

Extent of orange and number of eye-spots vary on both sides

♂

♀ often has pale band across underside hwing

♀ paler than ♂; eye-spots white-centred, enclosed within orange-yellow band

Both sexes have chequered fringes

A variable species, similar to the Arran brown (p 99); where the two fly together, the Large ringlet is distinguished by its smaller size. There are several subspecies; in some the orange bands are reduced to rings around the eye-spots. Widespread in coniferous forest zone of mountains from 1000 m up to timber line. *WS:* 42–46 mm; *Flight:* July–Aug; *Gen:* 1; *FP:* grasses; *D:* Cantabrians, Pyrenees, Alps, Balkans, Carpathians, Sudeten mts, Apennines, Yug.

Yellow-spotted ringlet

E. manto

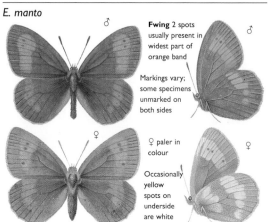

♂

Fwing 2 spots usually present in widest part of orange band

Markings vary; some specimens unmarked on both sides

♂

♀ paler in colour

Occasionally yellow spots on underside are white

♀

Many subspecies have been recorded for this variable butterfly, ranging from unmarked brown examples to those with well-developed upperside patterns. It may be found in damper parts of Alpine meadows, usually above 1000 m. *WS:* 34-44 m; *Flight:* June-Aug; *Gen:* 1; *FP:* various grasses; *D:* Pyrenees, Alps, Tatra mts, Balkans, Vosges mts.

Eriphyle ringlet

Erebia eriphyle ♂

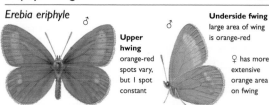

Upper hwing orange-red spots vary, but 1 spot constant

Underside fwing large area of wing is orange-red

♀ has more extensive orange area on fwing

Some variation occurs in this local Alpine species; specimens from the Bavarian Alps have brighter, better-defined markings, often enclosing black points. *WS:* 32–36 mm; *Flight:* July; *Gen:* 1; *FP:* unknown; *D:* Alps (Switz, S Germany, Austria).

White speck ringlet

E. claudina ♀

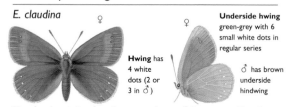

Hwing has 4 white dots (2 or 3 in ♂)

Underside hwing green-grey with 6 small white dots in regular series

♂ has brown underside hindwing

Very local; restricted to the grassy slopes of the eastern Alps above 1500 m. Distinguished from other ringlets by the white 'specks' on its hindwing. *WS:* 34–36 mm; *Flight:* July; *Gen:* 1; *FP:* grasses, esp *Deschampsia caespitosa*; *D:* Austria.

Mountain ringlet

E. epiphron ♂ ♀

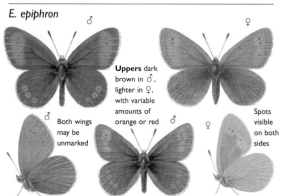

Uppers dark brown in ♂, lighter in ♀, with variable amounts of orange or red

Both wings may be unmarked

Spots visible on both sides

The specimens above are of *E. epiphron aetheria*, except for the lower central one, which is the British subspecies *mnemon*. The latter is very local and occurs only in central Scotland and the Lake District, usually above 500 m. There are many local European subspecies; generally they are dull brown with or without eyespots. *E. orientalis* is a similar species from Bulgaria. *WS:* 34–42 mm; *Flight:* June-Aug; *FP:* grasses; *D:* Europe (not Scand).

Yellow-banded ringlet

E. flavofasciata

♂

Underside hwing
wide yellow band
enclosing small black
spots diagnostic

♂

Spots clearer
on underside

Upper forewing
small red-ringed
black spots, arranged
in straight row

♀

♀ lighter brown, with spots often ringed in yellow

Underside bands
may be reduced
to row of yellow-
ringed spots

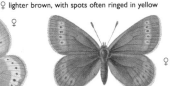

♀

An extremely local mountain species found only in a few isolated colonies in the Alps above 2000 m. *WS:* 34-36 mm; *Flight:* July; *Gen:* 1; *FP;* grasses; *D:* Switz, ? N Italy.
E. serotina (Descimon's ringlet) is a very rare butterfly recorded only from Cauterets in the Pyrenees. No females have ever been collected and the last specimens were seen about 20 years ago. It has a narrow red band on the topside with eye-spots which usually lack white centres, and is thought by some to be a hybrid of *E. epiphron* (p 102) and *E pronoe* (p 112). *WS:* 42–44 mm; *Flight:* Sept; *Gen:* 1; *FP:* unknown; *D:* SW France.

Blind (or Spotless) ringlet

E. pharte

♂

♂

Complete absence
of black spots from
both wing surfaces

♀ paler,
underside
suffused
yellowish

Upper fwing has
uniform band of
red oblong
spots; **hwing**
spots smaller,
more space in
between

♀

♀

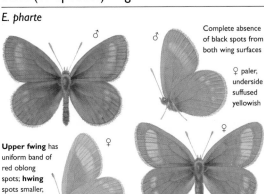

Known only from the Alps and Tatra mountains, this species does exhibit a certain amount of variation in its pattern, with some specimens almost unmarked and others with yellow rather than red spots. Found in mountain grassland above 1600 m. *WS:* 32–40 mm; *Flight:* July-Aug; *Gen:* 1; *FP:* unknown; *D:* Switz, SW France, S Germany, Austria, N Italy, Czech, Poland, Yug.

Rätzer's ringlet

Erebia christi

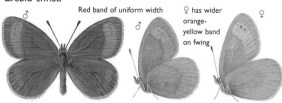

Red band of uniform width

♀ has wider orange-yellow band on fwing

♂ ♂ ♀

Similar to *E. epiphron* (p 102) but the underside hindwing has a pale outer area free of spots. Small colonies occur locally on mountains above 1400 m. *WS:* 36–40 mm; *Flight:* June–July; *Gen:* 1; *FP:* Sheep's fescue (*Festuca ovina*); *D:* S Switz.

Lesser mountain ringlet

E. melampus

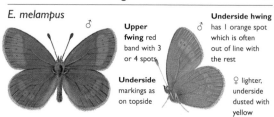

♂

Upper fwing red band with 3 or 4 spots

Underside markings as on topside

Underside hwing ♂ has 1 orange spot which is often out of line with the rest

♀ lighter, underside dusted with yellow

Specimens from high altitudes are often smaller and darker than those found lower down. A local species of Alpine valleys from 1000 to 2000 m. *WS:* 30–36 mm; *Flight:* June–Aug; *Gen:* 1; *FP:* grasses, esp *Poa*, *D:* SW France, Switz, N Italy, Austria.

Sudetan ringlet, *Erebia sudetica*, is similar to *E. melampus* but with marginal orange-brown bands and more regular markings. *WS:* 30–36 mm; *Flight:* July; *Gen:* 1; *FP:* unknown; *D:* S France, Germany, Romania.

Scotch argus

E. aethiops

3 white-centred eye-spots on forewing

Underside hwing has 4 white dots in pale grey band

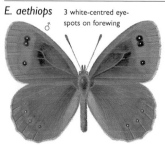 

♂ ♂

Velvety brown butterfly of variable size, found in open coniferous wood up to 1800 m. Active in sunshine. Female is brown and has yellowish bands enclosing bigger eye-spots. *WS:* 42–52 mm, *Flight:* Aug–Sept; *Gen:* 1; *FP:* grasses, esp *Molinia*; *D:* N Britain, E and C France, Belgium, Germany, Poland, Alps, Carpathians, Balkans.

de Prunner's ringlet

E. triaria

Fwing red band tapers towards hind margin ♂

3 apical spots touch ♂

Hwing dark, with paler outer area

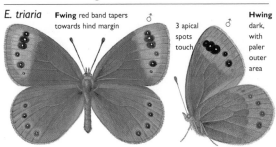

This ives in isolated colonies on grassy slopes up to 2500 m. *WS:* 44–50 mm; *Flight:* May–July; *Gen:* 1; *FP: Lolium, Poa*; *D:* Spain, Portugal, S and SE France, Switz, Austria, N Italy, Yug.

Lapland ringlet

E. embla

2 apical eye-spots join; often blind ♂

Upper hwing has 3 or 4 blind eye-spots, ringed in yellow

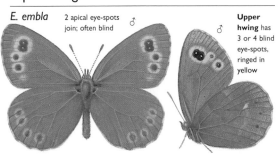

Locally common in lowland bogs near conifer woods. The female is usually paler, with more yellow around the eye-spots. *WS:* 50–52 mm; *Flight:* June–July; *Gen:* 1; *FP:* Sedge; *D:* Scand.

Arctic ringlet

E. disa

Apical spots blind, do not quite meet ♂

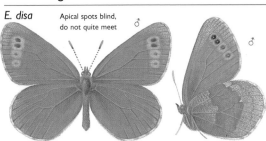

Distinguished from *E. embla* by absence of eye-spots on upper hindwing. Flies over wet moorland from sea level to 300 m, occurring most frequently along north coast of Scandinavia. *WS:* 46–50 mm; *Flight:* June–July; *Gen:* 1; *FP:* unknown; *D:* N Scand.

Woodland ringlet

Erebia medusa

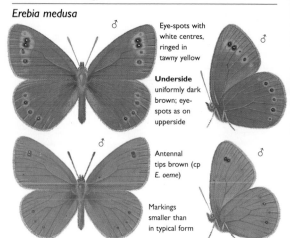

Eye-spots with white centres, ringed in tawny yellow

Underside uniformly dark brown; eye-spots as on upperside

Antennal tips brown (cp *E. oeme*)

Markings smaller than in typical form

E. medusa hippomedusa

There are generally four white-centred eye-spots, one between each vein, on the hindwing of this variable species. Several subspecies have been described based on size and number of these markings; in the subspecies illustrated they are very small, but in *psodea* they are larger and brighter than in the typical form. The females are paler than the males with larger spots surrounded by yellow. The butterfly lives in lowland bogs near woods in the north, but further south it is more of a mountain species. *WS:* 38–50 mm; *Flight:* May–July; *Gen:* 1; *FP:* grasses, esp *Digitaria, Milium; D:* C and E France, S Belgium, Germany, Poland, Austria, N Italy, Switz, Czech, Hungary, Yug, Romania, Bulgaria, Greece.

Arctic woodland ringlet

E. polaris

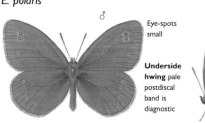 

Eye-spots small

Underside hwing pale postdiscal band is diagnostic

Formerly considered a subspecies of the Woodland ringlet but now regarded as a distinct species. It is very similar to *E. medusa hippomedusa* but has a more northerly distribution and the underside hindwing is not uniformly coloured. Found in dry, lightly wooded areas at low altitudes (rarely above 300 m). The female is paler with more distinct banding on the underside hindwing. *WS:* 40–44 mm; *Flight:* June–July; *Gen:* 1; *FP: Milium effusum,* Meadow grass (*Poa palvestris*); *D:* N Scand.

Almond-eyed ringlet

E. alberganus

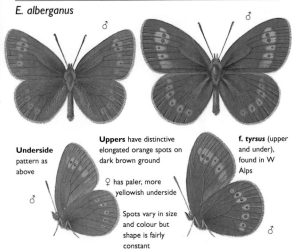

Underside pattern as above

Uppers have distinctive elongated orange spots on dark brown ground

♀ has paler, more yellowish underside

Spots vary in size and colour but shape is fairly constant

f. tyrsus (upper and under), found in W Alps

The almond-shaped spots on the upperside make this species identifiable, despite variations in colour and size. The form on the right is an example of a large specimen with bright markings; other forms may be smaller with vestigial orange spots. Found on mountain slopes from 1000 to 2000 m. *WS:* 40–46 mm; *Flight:* June–July; *Gen:* 1; *FP:* grasses, esp Meadow grass (*Poa*); *D:* N Spain, SE France, Switz, N and C Italy, Austria, Bulgaria, Yug.

Silky ringlet

E. gorge

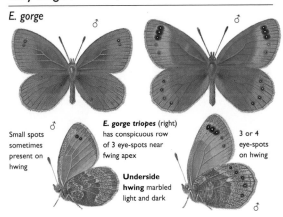

Small spots sometimes present on hwing

E. gorge triopes (right) has conspicuous row of 3 eye-spots near fwing apex

Underside hwing marbled light and dark

3 or 4 eye-spots on hwing

The red band on the forewing has a silky or gleaming texture. Many subspecies with different eye-spot combinations have been recorded; occasionally the spots are absent from both wings. Found on rocky slopes with little vegetation from 1500 to 3000 m. *WS:* 34–40 mm; *Flight:* June–July; *Gen:* 1; *FP:* grasses; *D:* Alps, Cantabrians, Pyrenees, Apennines, Balkans, Tatra mts, Yug.

Erebia pluto

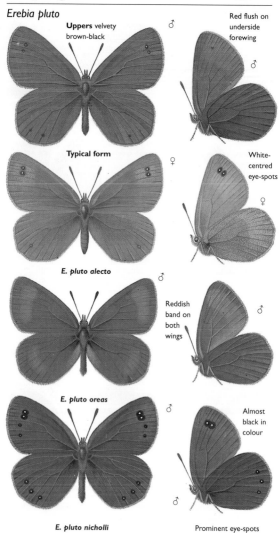

Uppers velvety brown-black ♂

Red flush on underside forewing ♂

Typical form ♀

White-centred eye-spots ♀

E. pluto alecto ♂

Reddish band on both wings ♂

E. pluto oreas ♂

Almost black in colour

E. pluto nicholli ♂

Prominent eye-spots

A dark-coloured butterfly with many named subspecies, some of which are illustrated above. The typical form is very distinctive in the field, the male having darker wings than the female, and it may be found on rocky mountainous terrain up to 2800 m. The various subspecies tend to be associated with different mountain ranges within the Alps, transitional forms occurring in intermediate areas. Generally they are distinguished by colour intensity and number of eye-spots. *WS:* 40–50 mm; *Flight:* June–Aug; *Gen:* 1; *FP:* grasses, esp Meadow Grass (*Poa*); *D:* Yug, Alps, Apennines (Switz, Austria, Italy, SE France).

Mnestra's ringlet

E. mnestra

♂ ♂

Eye-spots very small or absent

Underside hwing brown, unmarked

The female may be recognized by the presence of two small white-centred eye-spots on the forewing. This very local Alpine species occurs in small colonies on grassy mountain slopes between 1500 and 2000 m. *WS:* 34–38 mm; *Flight:* July; *Gen:* 1; *FP:* grasses; *D:* SE France, Austria, Switz, S Poland.

False mnestra ringlet

E. aethiopella

♂ ♂

Twin white-centred eye-spots usually present

Underside hwing has pale grey-brown band

The reddish band on the upper hindwing is more distinctive than in *E. mnestra* and the underside is well-marked in both sexes. This species flies over grassy slopes above 1800 m. *E. rhodopensis* is a similar, more heavily marked species from Bulgaria. *WS:* 36–40 mm; *Flight:* July–Aug; *Gen:* 1; *FP:* unknown, probably grasses; *D:* SE France, Switz, Bulgaria, S Yug.

Gavarnie ringlet

E. gorgone

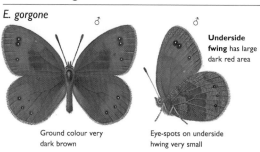

♂ ♂

Underside fwing has large dark red area

Ground colour very dark brown

Eye-spots on underside hwing very small

Small colonies occur at altitudes between 1800 and 2500 m on the grassy slopes of the Pyrenees. The female is paler than the male, with larger eye-spots and buff-coloured veins on the underside hindwing. *WS:* 40–42 mm; *Flight:* July–Aug; *Gen:* 1; *FP:* grasses, esp Meadow grass (*Pao*); *D:* N Spain, SW France.

Spring ringlet

Erebia epistygne

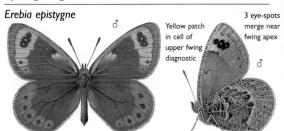

♂ Yellow patch in cell of upper fwing diagnostic

3 eye-spots merge near fwing apex ♂

The Spring ringlet is on the wing as early as March in hilly, lightly wooded areas up to 2000 m. The amount of yellow on the upper forewing is distinctive in both sexes. *WS:* 44–50 mm; *Flight:* Mar–June; *Gen:* 2; *FP:* grasses; *D:* S France, Spain.

Swiss brassy ringlet

E tyndarus

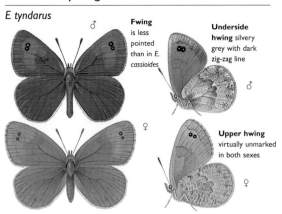

♂

Fwing is less pointed than in *E. cassioides*

♀

Underside hwing silvery grey with dark zig-zag line ♂

Upper hwing virtually unmarked in both sexes ♀

This local species is found on grass-covered Alpine slopes above 1800 m. The brassy ringlets are all very similar but rarely occur together in the same locality. *WS:* 34–36 mm; *Flight:* July–Aug; *Gen:* 1; *FP:* Mat grass (*Nardus stricta*); *D:* Alps.

De Lesse's brassy ringlet

E. nivalis

♂

Orange area on forewing extends further in towards wing base than in *E. tyndarus*

Underside hwing has bluish sheen ♂

The lack of eye-spots on the hindwing separates this species from *E. cassioides* (p 111). *WS:* 30–34 mm; *Flight:* July–Aug; *Gen:* 1; *FP:* Mat grass (*Nardus stricta*); *D:* Alps (Austria, Switz).

Common brassy ringlet

E. cassioides   ♂

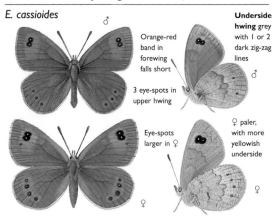

Orange-red band in forewing falls short

3 eye-spots in upper hwing

Underside hwing grey with 1 or 2 dark zig-zag lines

♂

Eye-spots larger in ♀

♀ paler, with more yellowish underside

♀

♀

The most widespread of the brassy ringlets, this species may be found on grassy slopes at around 1600 m. Each colony may exhibit small differences, and many forms and subspecies have been named as a result. *WS:* 32–38 mm; *Flight:* June–Aug; *Gen:* 1 (2?); *FP:* Mat grass (*Nardus stricta*); *D:* N Spain, France, Switz, Austria, Italy, Yug, Albania, Romania, Bulgaria.

Spanish brassy ringlet

E. hispania   ♂

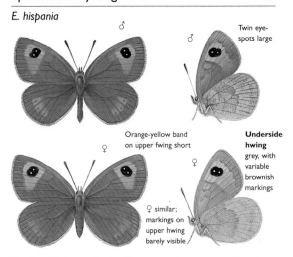

Twin eye-spots large

♂

Orange-yellow band on upper fwing short

♀

♀

Underside hwing grey, with variable brownish markings

♀ similar; markings on upper hwing barely visible

The Spanish brassy ringlet flies over rocky mountainsides above 2000 m. The subspecies *rondoui*, which is found in the Pyrenees, is small and more brightly marked. *WS:* 34–42 mm; *Flight:* June–July; *Gen:* 1; *FP:* unknown; *D:* S and N Spain, SW France. **E. calcaria** (Lorkovic's brassy ringlet) is very dark with small eye-spots. *WS:* 36-40 mm; *Flight:* July; *Gen:* 1; *FP:* grasses, esp *Festuca*; *D:* E Alps (Yug, NE Italy).

Ottoman brassy ringlet

Erebia ottomana

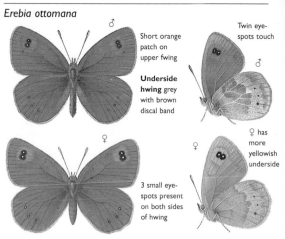

Short orange patch on upper fwing

Underside hwing grey with brown discal band

3 small eye-spots present on both sides of hwing

Twin eye-spots touch

♀ has more yellowish underside

The specimens above are subsp *tardenota* from the Massif Central, France; the more widespread subsp *balcanica* is distinguished by the absence of black spots on the underside hindwing. Found on grassy slopes above 1200 m. *WS:* 34–44 mm; *Flight:* July; *Gen:* 1; *FP:* unknown; *D:* C France, NE Italy, Yug, Bulgaria, Greece.

Water ringlet

E. pronoe

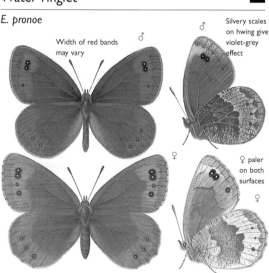

Width of red bands may vary

Silvery scales on hwing give violet-grey effect

♀ paler on both surfaces

The upperside markings vary; in some subsp the reddish band is faint and the eye-spots barely visible. It flies over damp slopes, often near woods, from 1000 to 1800 m. *WS:* 42–50 mm; *Flight:* July–Sept; *Gen:* 1; *FP: Poa; D:* Pyrenees, Alps, Balkans, Carpathians, Tatra mts.

Black ringlet

E. melas

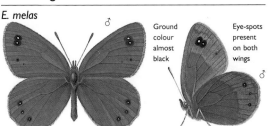

Ground colour almost black

Eye-spots present on both wings

The female has larger eye-spots, which are usually surrounded by orange. This species tends to live in limestone areas but little is known of its biology. *WS:* 42–48 mm; *Flight:* July–Aug; *Gen:* 1; *FP:* unknown; *D:* Romania, Yug, Greece.

Lefèbvre's ringlet

E. lefebvrei

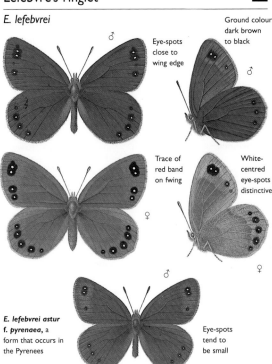

Eye-spots close to wing edge

Ground colour dark brown to black

Trace of red band on fwing

White-centred eye-spots distinctive

E. lefebvrei astur f. pyrenaea, a form that occurs in the Pyrenees

Eye-spots tend to be small

A mountain species, locally common above 1800 m in the Pyrenees and Cantabrian mountains. It is less brightly coloured than *E. meolans* (p 117), which flies in the same area, and is unlikely to be confused with *E. melas* as the latter is restricted to southeast Europe. *WS:* 40–48 mm; *Flight:* June–July; *Gen:* 1; *FP:* unknown, probably grasses; *D:* N Spain, SW France.

Larche ringlet

Erebia scipio

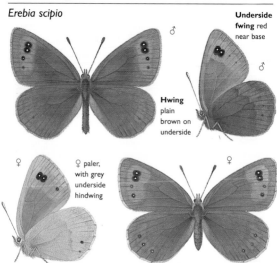

This very local species is becoming increasingly rare, having disappeared from some previous localities. It is found in high rocky areas above 1500 m. *WS:* 46–50 mm; *Flight:* June–Aug; *Gen:* 1; *FP:* unknown; *D:* S France, NW Italy (Alpes Maritimes).

Marbled ringlet

E. montana

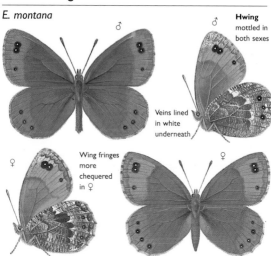

This is confined to Alps and Apennines above 1200 m. Subspecies above is *E. montana goante* from Switz and Austria; nominate is duller with more white on underside hwing. *WS:* 44–50 mm; *Flight:* July–Aug; *Gen:* 1; *FP:* grasses; *D:* S France, Austria, Italy, Switz.

Styrian ringlet

E stirius

Underside hwing dark brown with 3 white-centred eye-spots

Very similar to *E. styx*; *E. styrius* has a smoother underside hindwing and less red on the upperside. The underside hindwing of the female is grey-brown. *WS:* 46–52 mm; *Flight:* July–Sept; *Gen:* 1; *FP:* grasses; *D:* Austria, Switz, N Italy.

Stygian ringlet

E. styx

♀ is paler

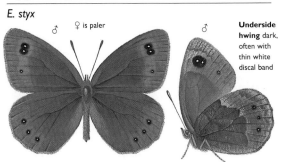

Underside hwing dark, often with thin white discal band

Essentially an Alpine butterfly, it flies at altitudes between 600 and 1800 m. Only recently regarded as a separate species from *E. styrius*. Several named subspecies. *WS:* 46–56 mm; *Flight:* July–Aug; *Gen:* 1; *FP:* grasses; *D:* Austria, Switz, N Italy, N Yug.

Autumn ringlet

E. neoridas

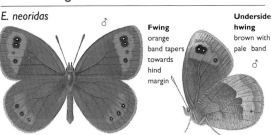

Fwing orange band tapers towards hind margin

Underside hwing brown with pale band

Found in mountainous areas from 600 to 1500 m. The female is generally paler on both wing surfaces with brighter upperside markings. *WS:* 36–46 mm; *Flight:* Aug–Sept; *Gen:* 1; *FP:* unknown; *D:* Spain (E Pyrenees), S France, Italy (Alps, Apennines).

Zapater's ringlet

Erebia zapateri

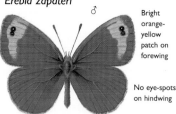

Bright orange-yellow patch on forewing

More orange on underside

No eye-spots on hindwing

This very local species is one of the few ringlets that is clearly recognizable in the field, on account of the bright coloration on its forewings. *WS:* 36–40 mm; *Flight:* July–Aug; *Gen:* 1; *FP:* Meadow grass (*Poa*), *Festuca*; *D:* C Spain.

Bright–eyed ringlet

E. oeme

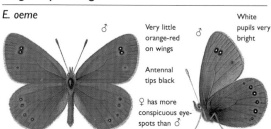

Very little orange-red on wings

Antennal tips black

♀ has more conspicuous eye-spots than ♂

White pupils very bright

In subspecies *lugens* the bright eye-spots are barely visible. May be found in damp meadows above 900 m. *WS:* 38–46 mm; *Flight:* June–July; *Gen:* 1; *FP:* Woodrush (*Luxula*) *D:* France, Pyrenees, Alps, Austria, Switz, Yug, Balkans, N Greece.

Chapman's ringlet

E. palarica

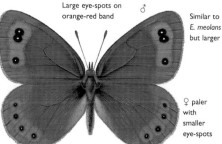

Large eye-spots on orange-red band

Similar to *E. meolans* but larger

Underside hwing mottled with white scales, giving rough appearance

♀ paler with smaller eye-spots

The larger size and rather rough underside hindwing distinguish this butterfly from the Piedmont ringlet (p 117). Very local in rough grassland areas of Spain. *WS:* 56–60 mm; *Flight:* June–July; *Gen:* 1; *FP:* Meadow grass (*Poa*), *Festuca*; *D:* NW Spain.

Piedmont ringlet

E. meolans

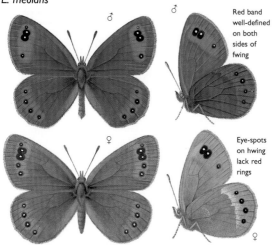

Red band well-defined on both sides of fwing

Eye-spots on hwing lack red rings

The Piedmont ringlet can be found on rocky mountain slopes from around 1000 to 1800 m. Several subspecies have been described based on variation in both the pattern and size; in Switzerland, subspecies *valesiaca* is smaller than the specimens illustrated, with reduced red markings and vestigial eye-spots. The female, besides being paler, usually has a grey postdiscal band on the underside hindwing. *WS:* 38–54 mm; *Flight:* May–July; *Gen:* 1; *FP:* grasses; *D:* N and C Spain, C and S France, C and N Italy, Switz, Austria, Germany.

Dewy ringlet

E. pandrose

 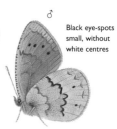

Black eye-spots small, without white centres

Orange area on fwing bordered or crossed by dark discal line

Underside hwing silvery grey with 2 wavy dark lines

In the southern part of its range this species flies in mountains above 1600 m, but further north it is a lowland insect. Female is similar to the male, except its underside hwing is yellowish grey. Dewy ringlet's pattern is not as variable as other ringlets'. *WS:* 40–50 mm; *Flight:* June–Aug; *Gen:* 1; *FP:* grasses; *D:* E Pyrenees, Alps, Apennines, Balkans, Carpathians, Scand (not Denmark).

False dewy ringlet

Erebia sthennyo

Underside hwing pale grey, almost unmarked

This butterfly is similar to the Dewy ringlet (p 117), but it is smaller and less widespread. Both occur in the Pyrenees above 1800 m, but generally not in the same places. *WS:* 40–44 mm; *Flight:* June–July; *Gen:* 1; *FP: Festuca*; *D:* N Spain, SW France.

Dalmatian ringlet

Proterebia afra

Underside hwing has eye-spots all round margin

Very local in eastern Europe, the Dalmatian ringlet is distinct from *Erebia* species. It flies over coastal cliffs and lower hill slopes in dry areas of Dalmatia. *WS:* 44–48 mm; *Flight:* May–June; *Gen:* 1; *FP:* unknown; *D:* Yug, S Russia.

Sardinian meadow brown

Maniola nurag

Prominent dark sex brand on ♂ forewing

♀ larger, more orange in colour than ♂

The Sardinian meadow brown is rather like a smaller, paler version of *M. jurtina hispulla* (p 119). It has a large amount of orange-yellow on both wings and occurs most frequently in the open areas of the northern part of the island. The adult females usually out-live the males. *WS:* 36–40 mm; *Flight:* June–July; *Gen:* 1; *FP:* grasses; *D:* Sardinia.

Meadow brown

M. jurtina

Single black, white-centred eye-spot

Uppers ♂ predominantly grey-brown, with very little orange. Dark sex brand visible under cell area of forewing

Underside fwing has large area of orange (both sexes)

Upper forewing ♀ has extensive orange-yellow markings

Light and dark areas on underside hwing more clearly defined in ♀

Large and very brightly coloured with prominent black eye-spot on forewing

M. jurtina hispulla, a subspecies found in S Europe

Probably one of the most common and widespread of the European butterflies, this species may be found throughout Britain and Ireland, especially in coastal areas. The extent of orange on the wings is variable and several subspecies have been described. *M. jurtina splendida*, for instance, from the west coast of Scotland, is brighter than the typical form, while the Irish subspecies *iernes* has a very plain underside. The Meadow brown can be found in a number of habitats from sea-level up to 1800 m, and is even known to occur in the centre of cities. It will fly in cloudy weather, but usually remains in a fairly restricted area. *WS:* 40–58 mm; *Flight:* June–Sept; *Gen:* 1–2; *FP:* grasses, esp Meadow grass (*Poa*); *D:* Europe (not N and C Scand).

Dusky meadow brown

Hyponephele lycaon

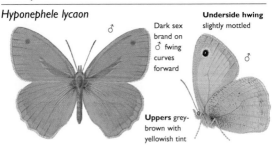

♂

Dark sex brand on ♂ fwing curves forward

Underside hwing slightly mottled

♂

Uppers grey-brown with yellowish tint

Female has large yellow area on upper fwing with two black spots. Slow, flapping flight in dry, stony lowlands. Population has declined. *WS:* 40–48 mm; *Flight:* June–Aug; *Gen:* 1; *FP:* grasses, esp *Poa*; *D:* S and C Europe (not Britain, Scand, Holland, Belgium, N France).

Oriental meadow brown

H. lupina

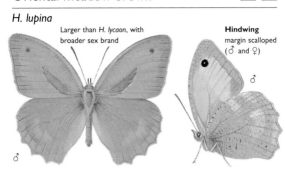

Larger than *H. lycaon*, with broader sex brand

Hindwing margin scalloped (♂ and ♀)

♂

♂

This is found on dry rocky hill slopes up to 1000 m. The female has two black spots ringed in orange on the upper forewing. *WS:* 42–48 mm; *Flight:* July–Aug; *Gen:* 1; *FP:* unknown; *D:* Spain, Portugal, S France, Italy, Sicily, Yug, Greece.

Southern gatekeeper

Pyronia cecilia

Sex brand on ♂ fwing rectangular, crossed by orange veins

Markings on underside more contrasting in ♀

Hwing lacks eye-spots on both sides

Similar to the Gatekeeper (p 121) except for differences in the male sex brand and the absence of eye-spots on the underside hindwing. Flies in hot, dry, scrubby areas. *WS:* 30–32 mm; *Flight:* May–Aug; *Gen:* 2 or more; *FP:* grasses, esp *Deschampsia*; *D:* Spain, Portugal, S France, Italy, Sicily, Yug, Greece.

Gatekeeper

P. tithonus

Fwing black eye-spot often has 2 white centres; sex brand prominent in ♂

♀ has larger, brighter orange areas on wings and lacks sex brand

Hindwing has dark basal area; underside yellowish with 2 or 3 eye-spots

Also known as the Hedge brown, probably because of the habitat in which it is found – hedgerows, fields and wooded lanes, especially where brambles are in bloom. Locally common and widespread, but in Britain it is confined mainly to southern and central areas. *WS:* 34–38 mm; *Flight:* July–Aug; *Gen:* 1; *FP:* Meadow grass (*Poa*), *Milium*, *D:* W, C and S Europe (not Scand, S Italy).

Spanish gatekeeper

P. bathseba

Fwing dark basal area obscures sex brand in ♂

Eye-spots on hwing ringed in yellow

Underside hwing brown with narrow yellow band

Flies in hot, dry areas up to 1500 m. *WS:* 36–38 mm; *Flight:* Apr–Aug; *Gen:* 2 +; *FP:* grasses; *D:* Portugal, S Spain, SW France.

Ringlet

Aphantopus hyperantus

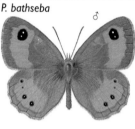

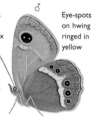

Conspicuous yellow-ringed eye-spots on underside

A very dark butterfly with a variable number of obscure eye-spots on the upperside. The female is paler and has larger, more regular markings. Found in damp, open woods, near hedgerows and also on sea cliffs. *WS:* 40–48 mm; *Flight:* June–Aug; *Gen:* 1; *FP:* grasses; *D:* Europe (not N Scand, S Spain, Italy).

Large heath

Coenonympha tullia

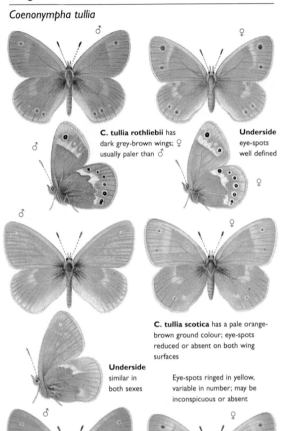

C. tullia rothliebii has dark grey-brown wings; ♀ usually paler than ♂

Underside eye-spots well defined

C. tullia scotica has a pale orange-brown ground colour; eye-spots reduced or absent on both wing surfaces

Underside similar in both sexes

Eye-spots ringed in yellow, variable in number; may be inconspicuous or absent

C. tullia thimoites (upperside only)

The Large heath is a northern butterfly with three subspecies in Britain: *rothliebii*, *scotica* and *thimoites*. All three may vary, and intermediate forms occur between isolated populations. The species is far less widespread than in previous years and is found on damp hillsides and swampy areas of moorlands. It has a heavy, slow flight. *WS:* 30–44 mm; *Flight:* June–July; *Gen:* 1; *FP:* Beaked rush (*Rhynchospora alba*); *D:* Britain, NE France, Scand, Belgium, Switz, N Germany, Czech, Austria, Poland.

C. rhodopensis (Eastern large heath) is more orange in colour and has a smaller white mark on the underside hindwing. *WS:* 32–34 mm; *Flight:* July; *Gen:* 1; *D:* Italy, SE Europe.

Corsican heath

C. corinna  ♂

Uppers bright orange with brown marginal borders

Underside fwing apical spot small, yellow-ringed; **hwing** wavy yellowish band

♂

Species has only been recorded in open grassy places. *WS:* 28-30 mm; *Flight:* May–Sept; *Gen:* 2-3; *FP:* unknown; *D:* Corsica, Sardinia. *C. elbana* (Elban heath) is similar but has better-developed eye-spots on the underside hindwing. *WS:* 24–28 mm; *Flight:* May–Sept; *Gen:* 2–3; *FP:* unknown; *D:* Elba.

Small heath

C. pamphilus ♂ 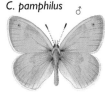 ♀

Uppers bright orange with narrow grey wing margins in both sexes

♂

Underside fwing has small black eye-spot, ringed in yellow

♀

Underside hwing has darker basal area followed by whitish band and indistinct eye-spots

A widespread butterfly with several subsp. It is easily distinguished from the Large heath (p 122) by its size and dark wing borders. It will fly up to 1800 m. *WS:* 26–34 mm; *Flight:* May–Sept; *Gen:* 2 (more in south); *FP:* grasses; *D:* Europe (not N Scand).
Cretan heath, *Coenonympha thyrsis*. Upperside with darker margin than *C. pamphilus*; hwing fringe has distinct black ladder-like markings. Underside pale with well-defined dark zig-zag. *WS:* 30–32 mm; *Flight:* April–Sept; *Gen:* 2; *FP:* unknown; *D:* Crete, Sicily.

Alpine heath

C. gardetta ♂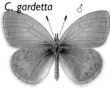

 ♂

Forewing has slight orange flush

Hindwing dusky brown, poorly marked

Black eye-spots without rings in white band on underside hwing

A local but often abundant species in high Alpine meadows up to 2100 m. In some specimens the upperside is plain grey and lacks any orange on the forewing. *WS:* 30–32 mm; *Flight:* July–Aug; *Gen:* 1; *FP:* unknown; *D* Switz, Austria, S Germany, N Italy, Yug.

Dusky heath

Coenonympha dorus

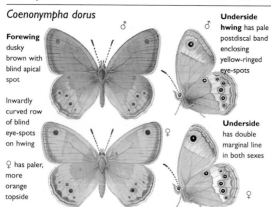

♂

Forewing dusky brown with blind apical spot

Inwardly curved row of blind eye-spots on hwing

♀ has paler, more orange topside

♂

Underside hwing has pale postdiscal band enclosing yellow-ringed eye-spots

Underside has double marginal line in both sexes

♀

A very variable species, often locally common in dry, rocky areas up to 1800 m. *WS:* 28–34 mm; *Flight:* June–July; *Gen:* 1; *FP:* grasses; *D:* Spain, Portugal, S France, N and C Italy.

Pearly heath

C. arcania

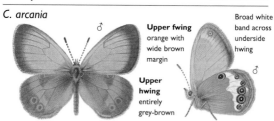

♂

Upper fwing orange with wide brown margin

Upper hwing entirely grey-brown

Broad white band across underside hwing

♂

Found on grassy slopes between 1200 and 1800 m. The females are often less common than the males. *WS:* 34–40 mm; *Flight:* June–July; *Gen:* 1; *FP:* grasses; *D:* Europe (not Britain, N Scand). *C. darwiniana* (Darwin's heath) is smaller, with a narrower, more even white band on the underside hindwing. Flies at 1500 m. *WS:* 32–34 mm; *Flight:* July–Aug; *Gen:* 1; *D:* Alps.

False ringlet

C. oedippus

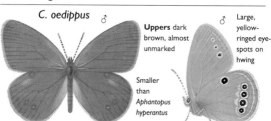

♂

Uppers dark brown, almost unmarked

Smaller than *Aphantopus hyperantus*

♂

Large, yellow-ringed eye-spots on hwing

WS: 34–42 mm; *Flight:* June–July; *Gen:* 1; *FP:* Sedge (*Carex*); *D:* SW and C France, N Italy, Belgium (rare), Austria, Hungary, Yug.

Russian heath

C. leander

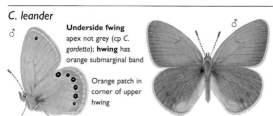

♂

Underside fwing apex not grey (cp *C. gardetta*); **hwing** has orange submarginal band

Orange patch in corner of upper hwing

♂

In the female the orange patch on the upper hindwing spreads out more and the forewings are flushed yellow-buff. It is more widespread in Asia than in Europe, and is found on grasslands up to 1500 m. *WS:* 32–34 mm; *Flight:* May–July; *Gen:* 1; FL: Meadow grass (*Poa*), *Festuca*; *D:* NE Greece, Romania, Bulgaria, S Russia.

Scarce heath

C. hero

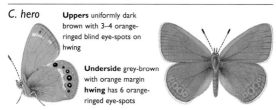

Uppers uniformly dark brown with 3–4 orange-ringed blind eye-spots on hwing

Underside grey-brown with orange margin **hwing** has 6 orange-ringed eye-spots

Local and comparatively rare, with widely dispersed colonies. It favours damp, open terrain. *WS:* 30–34 mm; *Flight:* May–June; *Gen:* 1; *FP:* grasses (*Lolium, Carex*); *D:* S Scand, Belgium, NE France, Holland, Germany, Czech, Poland, Baltic states.

Chestnut heath

C. glycerion

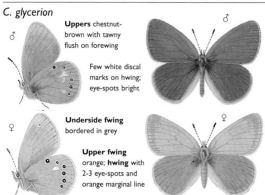

♂

Uppers chestnut-brown with tawny flush on forewing

Few white discal marks on hwing; eye-spots bright

♂

♀

Underside fwing bordered in grey

Upper fwing orange; **hwing** with 2-3 eye-spots and orange marginal line

♀

Isolated colonies of the Chestnut heath are found in damp meadowland up to 1500 m. *WS:* 32–46 mm; *Flight:* June–July; *Gen:* 1; *FP:* grasses; *D:* Yug, C and E Europe (not Britain, NW France, Scand, Spain, Portugal, Belgium, Holland, S Italy, Greece).

Spanish heath

Coenonympha iphioides ♂

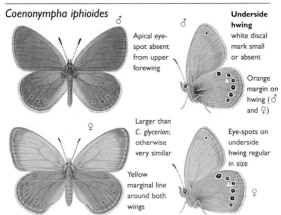

Apical eye-spot absent from upper forewing

♂

Underside hwing
white discal mark small or absent

Orange margin on hwing (♂ and ♀)

Larger than *C. glycerion*; otherwise very similar

Eye-spots on underside hwing regular in size

Yellow marginal line around both wings

Sometimes listed as a subspecies of the Chestnut heath (p 125) it is smaller with less conspicuous markings. The Spanish heath flies over grassy slopes up to 1700 m. *WS:* 34–40 mm; *Flight:* June–July; *Gen:* 1; *FP: Bracypodium, Melica; D:* N and C Spain.

Speckled wood

Pararge aegeria ♂

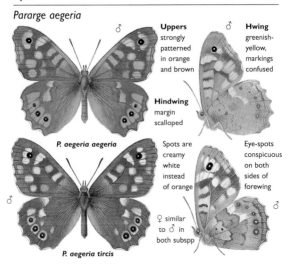

Uppers
strongly patterned in orange and brown

♂

Hwing
greenish-yellow, markings confused

Hindwing
margin scalloped

P. aegeria aegeria

Spots are creamy white instead of orange

Eye-spots conspicuous on both sides of forewing

♀ similar to ♂ in both subspp

P. aegeria tircis

The typical form, *P. aegeria aegeria*, occurs mainly in southern Europe; further north, including Britain, it is replaced by *P. aegeria tircis*. The butterfly has a slow, fluttering flight and is commonly found in shady areas with dappled sunlight, such as woodland edges and pine-forest clearings, where its spotted pattern blends in well with the surroundings. *WS:* 38–44 mm; *Flight:* Mar–Oct; *Gen:* 2 or more (1 in Scand); *FP:* grasses, esp Couch grass (*Agropyron*); *D:* Europe (not N Scand, N Scot).

Large wall brown

Lasiommata maera

L. petropolitana (below) is smaller, with a wavy discal band across hwing

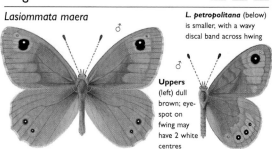

Uppers (left) dull brown; eye-spot on fwing may have 2 white centres

Often common in forest clearings. *WS:* 44–54 mm; *Flight:* May–Sept; *Gen:* 2; *FP:* grasses; *D:* Europe (not Britain, N Scand). **L. petropolitana** (Northern wall brown). *WS:* 38–42 mm; *Flight:* May–Sept; *Gen:* 1–2; *FP:* grasses, esp *Festuca*; *D:* Alps, Pyrenees, Scand, Bulgaria, SE Yug, Greece.

Wall brown

L. megera

Uppers orange-yellow with brown criss-cross pattern

Upperside hwing grey with intricate markings

♀ larger, paler

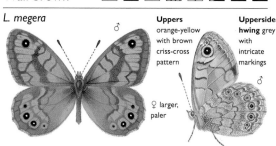

Fluttery in flight; settles on bare soil to bask in the sun. A widespread species, found on rough open ground and along hedgerows. *WS:* 36–50 mm; *Flight:* Mar–Sept; *Gen:* 2–3; *FP:* grasses, esp Meadow grass (*Poa*); *D:* Europe (not N Scand, N Scot).

Woodland brown

L. achine

Ground colour greyish brown, paler on underside

Row of large yellow-ringed black spots on both wings

♀ similar, often paler with slightly bigger spots

Widely scattered colonies occur in open woodland up to 1000 m. *WS:* 50–56 mm; *Flight:* June–July; *Gen:* 1; *FP:* grasses; *D:* France, Germany, Baltic states, S Sweden, N Italy, Yug.

Lattice brown

Lasiommata roxelana

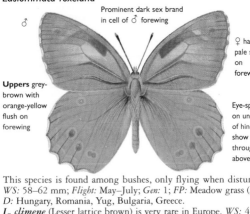

Prominent dark sex brand in cell of ♂ forewing

♂

♀ has pale spots on forewing

Uppers grey-brown with orange-yellow flush on forewing

Eye-spots on underside of hindwing show through from above

This species is found among bushes, only flying when disturbed. *WS:* 58–62 mm; *Flight:* May–July; *Gen:* 1; *FP:* Meadow grass (*Poa*); *D:* Hungary, Romania, Yug, Bulgaria, Greece.
L. climene (Lesser lattice brown) is very rare in Europe. *WS:* 46-48 mm; *Flight:* June-July; *Gen:* 1; *FP:* unknown; *D:* SE Europe.

Metalmarks Riodinidae (Nemeobiidae)

Most of the Riodinidae occur in South America and include some very colourful species. Closely related to the Blues (Lycaenidae), they are distinguished by the reduced forelegs of the male (but not female), which are useless for walking. In Europe this family is represented by one species, the Duke of Burgundy fritillary.

Caterpillar of the Duke of Burgundy fritillary

Eggs laid on underside of cowslip leaves. Caterpillar eats most of eggshell on hatching, then continues to feed on leaf underside

Pale fawn woodlouse-shaped body, spotted and covered in short hairs

Duke of Burgundy fritillary

Hamearis lucina

♂

Wings of ♀ not as pointed as in ♂, and orange markings wider

♀

♀

Northern specimens are small, single-brooded. **Underside hwing** has 2 rows of white spots

Uppers dark brown with transverse rows of orange spots; in 2nd generation these spots are smaller

The butterfly's name is a misnomer as it bears only a superficial resemblance to the fritillary. Widespread but rarely common, it is found in woodland clearings. *WS:* 28–34 mm; *Flight:* May–June, Aug; *Gen:* 2; *FP:* Cowslip, Primrose (*Primula*); *D:* Europe; incl S Sweden (not rest of Scand, Ireland, Holland, S Spain).

Blues, Hairstreaks and Coppers Lycaenidae

This is a large family of worldwide distribution, with about 100 species in Europe and many more in the rainforests of Asia and Africa. They are normally small, metallic-coloured butterflies with marked differences between the sexes; the males are often blue or coppery, while the females are usually brown. However, both sexes have similar markings on the underside, and it is from these delicate patterns (especially on the hindwings) that the species are identified. Of the three groups into which the Lycaenidae are divided, the Blues are by far the most numerous and may be seen in abundance on chalk downs in the summer (although they are not as common as in previous years). The Hairstreaks are usually recognized by the fine hairline markings on the underside, while the Coppers are unmistakable in their brilliant coloration. Most of these butterfiles are quick in flight and tend to settle when the sun goes in.

Chalkhill blue caterpillar

Ants attracted to sweet secretion from honey gland

Feeds on vetches. Yellow stripes and black dots on green, rather slug-like body

Brown hairstreak

Thecla betulae

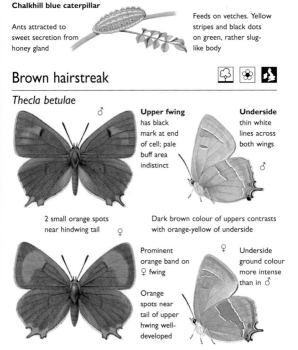

♂

Upper fwing has black mark at end of cell; pale buff area indistinct

Underside thin white lines across both wings ♂

2 small orange spots near hindwing tail ♀

Dark brown colour of uppers contrasts with orange-yellow of underside

Prominent orange band on ♀ fwing

♀ **Underside** ground colour more intense than in ♂

Orange spots near tail of upper hwing well-developed

This butterfly tends to fly in short, sharp bursts, fairly high up, and only when the sun is shining. It is mainly a woodland species, but may also fly near hedgerows and in open spaces. Its occurrence very much depends on the proximity of foodplants, upon which the eggs are laid singly in the autumn, and remain without hatching until spring. In southern England and Wales the species is widely distributed but rather local, and is unlikely to be seen unless one purposely searches in a probable area. *WS:* 34–36 mm; *Flight:* Aug–Sept; *Gen:* 1; *FP:* Sloe (*Prunus spinosa*) and others; *D:* Europe (not Scot, N Ireland, N Scand, S Spain, S Portugal, S Italy, Mediterranean islands).

Spanish purple hairstreak

Laeosopis roboris

Purplish-blue area spreads out from wing base; borders wide, dark

Smaller patch of purple on hindwing

Pointed black marks edged with white on hindwing

♂

The wings of the female are more rounded and the amount of purple is restricted to the base of the forewing. Locally common where ash trees occur, up to 1500 m. In parts of Spain it may reach pest proportions. *WS:* 24–30 mm; *Flight:* May–Aug; *Gen:* 1–2; *FP:* Ash (*Fraximus excelsior*); *D:* SE France, Spain, Portugal.

Purple hairstreak

Quercusia quercus

♂

Uppers deep purple or violet-blue, with dark borders

Prominent white line on greyish background

♀

♀ is dark brown, with shiny violet area on fwing, less extensive than in ♂

Orange-yellow spots near corner of hindwing

The iridescent purple varies according to the way the light falls on the wings. An oakwood species, flying mainly in the tree tops; in some years it is very common. The caterpillar resembles the leaf buds on which it feeds. *WS:* 24–28 mm; *Flight:* July–Sept; *Gen:* 1–2; *FP:* Oak (*Quercus*); *D:* Europe (local in Ireland; not N Scand, N Scot).

Sloe hairstreak

Satyrium acaciae

Uppers dark brown, unmarked except for orange spot near tail of hindwing

♂

Underside light brown with orange marginal marks on hindwing

♂

Found on rough ground near sloe bushes, up to 1500 m. *WS:* 28–32 mm; *Flight:* June–July; *Gen:* 1; *FP:* Sloe (*Prunus spinosa*); *D:* Spain, France, Switz, S Germany, Italy, Balkans, Greece.

Ilex hairstreak

S. ilicis

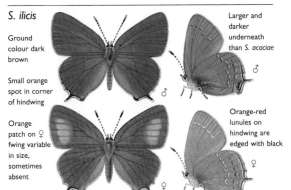

Ground colour dark brown

Small orange spot in corner of hindwing

Orange patch on ♀ fwing variable in size, sometimes absent

Larger and darker underneath than *S. acaciae*

♂

Orange-red lunules on hindwing are edged with black

♀

An active but inconspicuous butterfly, locally common on hills with small oaks. *WS:* 32–36 mm; *Flight:* July; *Gen:* 1; *FP:* Oak (*Quercus*); *D:* Europe (not Britain, N Scand; rare in S Spain).

False ilex hairstreak

S. esculi

Uppers resemble ♂ *N. ilicis;* often more grey-brown in colour

Bright orange-red lunules on hwing faintly edged with black

♂

The female may have an orange tinge on the upper forewing, but not as distinctive as the orange patch on the Ilex hairstreak. Found on hillsides with bushes. *WS:* 30–34 mm; *Flight:* June–July; *Gen:* 1; *FP:* Oak (*Quercus*); *D:* Spain, Portugal, S France.

Provence hairstreak

Tomares ballus

Light grey-brown pointed wings

Large areas of orange-yellow on ♀ uppers

Green hwing (both sexes)

Found on rough, stony ground. *WS:* 28–30 mm; *Flight:* Jan–Apr: *Gen:* 1; *FP:* Trefoil (*Lotus*); *D:* Spain, Portugal, S France. *T. nogelli* (Nogel's hairstreak) is darker with grey and orange bands edged with black dots, on underside hindwing. *WS:* 30–32 mm; *Flight:* May–June; *FP:* Vetch (*Astragalus*); *D:* Romania.

Blue-spot hairstreak

Satyrium spini ♂

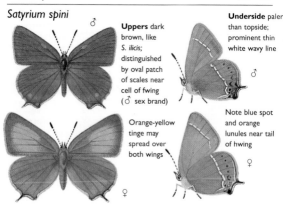

Uppers dark brown, like *S. ilicis*; distinguished by oval patch of scales near cell of fwing (♂ sex brand)

Orange-yellow tinge may spread over both wings

Underside paler than topside; prominent thin white wavy line ♂

Note blue spot and orange lunules near tail of hwing ♀

f. *vandalusica* a ♀ form found in Spain (uppers and unders)

The typical female, apart from being slightly larger and more distinctly marked, is much more like the male in colour than the form *vandalusica*. this name is derived from the blue spot on the underside of the hindwing: Widespread in hilly, uncultivated scrubland up to 1800 m; rare in the northern part of its range. *WS:* 28–32 mm; *Flight:* June–July; *Gen:* 1; *FP:* Buckthorn (*Rhaminus*), Sloe (*Prunus spinosa*); *D:* Europe (not Britain, Scand, Holland, Belgium).

Black hairstreak

S. pruni

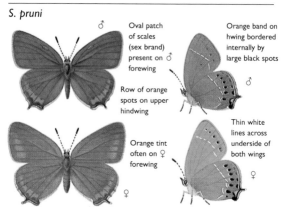

Oval patch of scales (sex brand) present on ♂ forewing

Row of orange spots on upper hindwing

Orange tint often on ♀ forewing

Orange band on hwing bordered internally by large black spots ♂

Thin white lines across underside of both wings ♀

The black spots which border the orange band on the underside hindwing are a characteristic feature of this butterfly. It is usually found near hedgerows and in open woodland, especially where old sloe bushes have been allowed to grow unchecked. In Britain the species is declining and is known to occur only in a few localities in the Midlands. It is more widespread (but rarely common) in central Europe. *WS:* 30–32 mm; *Flight:* June–July; *Gen:* 1; *FP:* Sloe (*Prunus spinosa*); *D:* C and E Europe, including N Spain (not Portugal, Ireland, Norway, peninsular Italy, Holland, Belgium).

White-letter hairstreak

S. w-album

♂

Sexes are separated by oval sex brand on ♂ forewing

Underside thin white line forms distinct W-shape on hindwing

♂

Ground colour dark brown; ♀ slightly paler

May be confused with Black hairstreak (p 132), but is paler on the underside and lacks orange spots on the upper hindwing. Often near elms, feeding at bramble flowers in hedgerows. Widespread, in Britain it is locally common in the south (incl Wales). *WS:* 30–34 mm; *Flight:* June–Aug; *Gen:* 1–2; *FP:* Elm (*Ulmus*), Lime (*Tilia*); *D:* Europe (rare Holland, not Ireland, N Scand, Portugal, S Spain).

Green hairstreak

Callophrys rubi

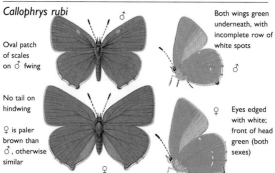

♂

Oval patch of scales on ♂ fwing

Both wings green underneath, with incomplete row of white spots

♂

No tail on hindwing

♀ is paler brown than ♂, otherwise similar

Eyes edged with white; front of head green (both sexes)

♀

The only other similar European species is *C. avis*. It has a short, rapid flight and is well-camouflaged when at rest on green leaves. Occurs in a wide range of habitats, from woodland to moorland bogs, and has many suitable foodplants. *WS:* 26–30 mm; *Flight:* Mar–June; *Gen:* 1; *FP:* Leguminosae; *D:* Europe.

Chapman's green hairstreak

C. avis

♂

Resembles *C. rubi*, but front of head and edge of eyes reddish brown

Sexes are similar

Continuous white line (broken at veins) across both wings

♂

Principally North African, its topside tends to be more red-brown than *C. rubi*. *WS:* 32–34 mm; *Flight:* Apr–May; *Gen:* 1–2; *FP:* Strawberry tree (*Arbutus unedo*); *D:* S France, Spain, Portugal.

Violet copper

Lycaena helle — Violet dust covering ♂ upperside obscures orange-brown pattern clearly visible on ♀

♂

♀

Prominent orange marginal band on both sides of hindwing (♂ and ♀)

The male is very distinctive but the female lacks the violet colour. Colonies tend to be local and isolated, in areas of wet meadowland, often near forests. *WS:* 24–28 mm; *Flight:* May–Oct; *Gen:* 1–2; *FP:* Knotgrass (*Polygonum*); *D:* Scand (not Denmark, S Sweden), Germany, Switz, Belgium, Poland, Czech.

Small copper

L. phlaeas

♂

Upper fwing golden red with black spots and dark border

Upper hwing predominantly dark grey with orange margin

Underside hwing brown with small dark spots and reddish marginal marks

♂

The female is similar but has more rounded wings. Widespread throughout Europe (except the north of Scotland), this bright little butterfly is often seen in flowery meadows. *WS:* 24–30 mm; *Flight:* Mar–Oct; *Gen:* 3; *FP:* Dock, Sorrel (*Rumex* spp.); *D:* Europe.

Large copper

L. dispar

♀ darker, with wide margins and more spots than ♂

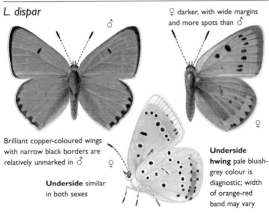

♂

♀

Brilliant copper-coloured wings with narrow black borders are relatively unmarked in ♂

♀

Underside similar in both sexes

Underside hwing pale bluish-grey colour is diagnostic; width of orange-red band may vary

♀

Swamp drainage caused this species to decline. English subspecies became extinct over a century ago, and has been replaced by Dutch subspecies *batavus*, introduced to East Anglia in 1927. *WS:* 34–40 mm; *Flight:* May–June; *Gen:* 1; *FP:* Water dock (*Rumex*); *D:* Austria, England, France, Italy, Holland, Germany, Baltic states, Balkans.

Scarce copper

L. virgaureae

♂ has coppery wings without black spots; ♀ heavily marked, lacks lustre of ♂

Wing fringes yellowish-grey

Underside similar in both sexes

Underside hwing yellow-brown with small black spots; white markings in postdiscal area are characteristic

L. virgaureae miegii, a Spanish subspecies, has wider black borders than the typical form

Small black spots present on upperside

♀ of this subsp has markings like the ♀ above, but without as much dark diffusion

Chiefly a central European species with colonies extending westward, the Scarce copper exhibits considerable variation over its range. It has a fast, steady flight and is locally common in flowery meadows up to 1500 m. *WS:* 30–36 mm; *Flight:* July–Aug; *Gen:* 1; *FP:* Dock (*Rumex*); *D:* N and C Europe, incl isolated colonies in Spain and Portugal (not Britain, Holland, Belgium, N Scand).

Sooty copper

L. tityrus

Uppers dark grey-brown with indistinct orange marks near margins

Underside greenish-grey with small black spots and orange marginal band

Fwing orange, with black spots

Hwing round black marginal spots barely touch edge

Orange flush sometimes visible on fwing (♂ and ♀)

Unlike other coppers, the male Sooty copper is not a beautiful burnished colour but more of a sooty brown. Several subspecies have been described, some of which are more orange-red on the topside. Usually in flowery meadows or in drier areas near forests, up to 2000 m. *WS:* 28–32 mm; *Flight:* Apr–Sept; *Gen:* 2; *FP:* Dock (*Rumex*); *D:* Europe, incl S Denmark (not Britain, Scand, S Spain).

Purple-shot copper

Lycaena alciphron

Wings of ♀ broad, dark brown, with darker spots

Uppers copper colour obscured by purple scales; spots indistinct

Pattern of spots well-defined on underside

Underside (♂ and ♀) grey with numerous black spots and orange band on hwing

Underside forewing flushed with orange in ♀

♂ **L. alciphron gordius**   ♀ **L. alciphron gordius**

A widespread species found in warm flowery meadows from lowlands up to 1800 m. The row of postdiscal spots on the upper forewing of the female is uneven, and this serves as a distinction from the Purple-edged copper (p 138). The amount of purple on the wings varies, as shown in subsp *gordius*, which occurs in the mountains of southern Europe. Here both sexes have more copper colour showing through on the topside, and the markings are larger. *WS:* 32–36 mm; *Flight:* June–July; *Gen:* 1; *FP:* Dock (*Rumex*); *D:* Europe (not Britain, Scand, Holland, Belgium).

Grecian copper

L. ottomanus

Uppers gleaming golden red with wide black borders

Like *L. virgaureae*, but no white spots on underside hwing; red lunules distinct

The wings of the female are not dissimilar to the Scarce copper (p 135) on the upperside. Small, local colonies are generally found in flowery meadows. *WS:* 28–30 mm; *Flight:* Mar–July; *Gen:* 2; *FP:* unknown; *D:* Greece, Albania, Yug.

Lesser fiery copper

L. thersamon

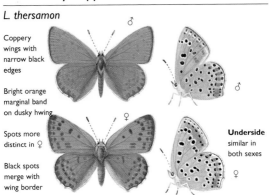

Coppery wings with narrow black edges

Bright orange marginal band on dusky hwing

Spots more distinct in ♀

Black spots merge with wing border

Underside similar in both sexes

Specimens of the second generation often have a slight tail on the hindwing. The duskiness on the upperside tends to vary; some dark females may be confused with the Sooty copper (p 135), but are distinguished by the marginal spots on the upper hindwing which fuse with the dark border. It is more common in eastern Europe, in areas of uncultivated ground up to 1200 m. *WS:* 28–32 mm; *Flight:* Apr–Aug; *Gen:* 2; *FP:* Dock (*Rumex*), Broom (*Sarothamnus*); *D:* Italy, Austria, Czech, Hungary, Romania, Greece, Balkans.

Long-tailed blue

Lampides boeticus

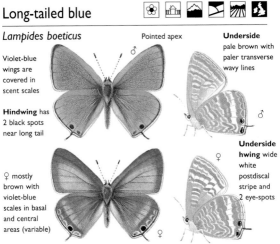

Pointed apex

Underside pale brown with paler transverse wavy lines

Violet-blue wings are covered in scent scales

Hindwing has 2 black spots near long tail

Underside hwing wide white postdiscal stripe and 2 eye-spots

♀ mostly brown with violet-blue scales in basal and central areas (variable)

The Long-tailed blue flies so quickly that it is often difficult to see. It is strongly migratory and occasionally reaches Britain from its breeding grounds in the south. Its distribution is virtually worldwide, and in certain parts it is a serious crop pest, as the caterpillar actually lives inside the pods of Leguminosae. It scurs in many habitats, usually with rich vegetation, up to 2000 m. *WS:* 30–36 mm; *Flight:* May–Sept; *Gen:* 2–3; *FP:* Leguminosae, esp *Colutea*, *Croatalaria*; *D:* S Europe (migrates north).

Purple-edged copper

Lycaena hippothoe

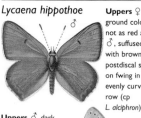

Uppers ♀
ground colour
not as red as
♂, suffused
with brown,
postdiscal spots
on fwing in
evenly curved
row (cp
L. *alciphron*)

Uppers ♂ dark
orange-red with black
borders, shot with
purple, esp around
fwing costa and
on hwing

Underside (both
sexes) grey with
spots in typical
pattern; amount of
orange may vary

A complex of several geographically distinct species in Europe under the name *L. hippothoe*, including the related species, *candens*. A variable species; the subsp *eurydame*, occurring south of the Rhône, lacks a violet tinge and is more golden in the male (female mostly brown). Widespread but local, becoming rarer; flies in wet meadows up to 2000 m. *WS:* 32–38 mm; *Flight:* June–July; *Gen:* 1; *FP:* Dock (*Rumex*); *D:* Europe (not Britain, S Spain, NW France, Holland).

Fiery copper

L. thetis

Intense fiery
red colour on
wings; black
border widest
at fwing apex

Underside hwing
greyish with obscure
yellow marginal band

The female is less intensely coloured and has typical spot markings above. Both sexes have a thin tail on the hindwing. A rare mountain species, attracted to thyme. *WS:* 30–32 mm; *Flight:* July; *Gen:* 1; *FP:* unknown; *D:* Greece, Yug (?).

Lang's short-tailed blue

Syntarucus pirithous

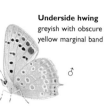

Uppers violet-
blue in ♂; grey-
brown in ♀

Basal area
bluish

Underside
brown with
wavy pattern
of white lines

The variable underside pattern lacks the broad white stripe seen on the Long-tailed blue (p. 137). Locally common in rough pastures near the sea. *WS:* 24–26 mm; *Flight:* Mar–Sept; *Gen:* 2–3; *FP:* Leguminosae; *D:* S Europe (all Mediterranean countries).

Common tiger blue

Tarucus theophrastus

Uppers
purplish
blue with black
mark in cell of
forewing

Uppers brown
with white
spots; pattern
on underside
shows through

Underside white
with black lines
and spots; row of
discrete postdiscal
spots across
both wings

Underside
markings as in ♂

The Common tiger blue occurs only locally in Europe, being more widespread in North Africa. It flies in hot, dry localities at low altitudes, often near the coast, in the vicinity of its foodplant. *WS:* 20–22 mm; *Flight:* Apr–Sept; *Gen:* 3 or more; *FP:* Jujube bush (*Ziziphus vulgaris*); *D:* S Spain.

Little tiger blue

T. balkanicus

Uppers purplish-
blue with dark
spots on forewing

Uppers brown
with dusting of
blue scales in basal
area; no white
spots on forewing

Underside white
with black spots as
in *T. theophrastus*,
but postdiscal
spots form
continuous line

Sexes are similar
underneath

The distribution of this species is not well known, as it has often been mistaken for the Common tiger blue. It can be distinguished, however, by its smaller size and upperside markings. Prefers hot, dry lowlands. *WS:* 18–22 mm; *Flight:* Apr–Sept; *Gen:* 2–3; *FP:* Christ's thorn (*Paliurus spina-christi*); *D:* Greece, Yug, Bulgaria, Albania.

African grass blue

Zizeeria knysna

Violet-blue wings
with wide brown
borders; ♀ brown

Underside
grey-brown
with small dark
spots; ♀ similar

Two very similar subspecies of the African grass blue occur in Europe; one in Sicily and Crete, the other in isolated colonies in the Iberian peninsula. They both live in damp, marshy meadows, often near streams, at low altitudes. *WS:* 20–24 mm; *Flight:* Apr–Aug; *Gen:* 2; *FP:* Medick (*Medicago*); *D:* Spain, Portugal, Sicily, Crete.

Short-tailed blue

Cupido argiades

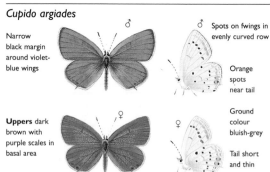

Narrow black margin around violet-blue wings

Spots on fwings in evenly curved row

Orange spots near tail

Uppers dark brown with purple scales in basal area

Ground colour bluish-grey

Tail short and thin

This rare migrant to Britain was once known as the 'Bloxworth blue' because it was first recorded from near Bloxworth in Dorset. In southern Europe it is locally common in damp meadows up to 1000 m. The second-generation male is darker blue. *WS:* 20–30 mm; *Flight:* Apr–Sept; *Gen:* 2 or more; *FP:* Medick (*Medicago*), Trefoil (*Lotus*); *D:* Europe (not S and C Spain, Norway, Sweden; migrant to Britain, N Germany, Holland, Denmark, Finland).

Eastern short-tailed blue

C. decoloratus

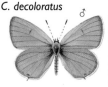

Small black mark at top of cell in upper fwing

Underside pale grey with small scattered spots

Lighter in colour than *C. argiades*

No orange on hwing

A brighter blue when it first emerges; the dark scales around the edges and along the veins become more noticeable with age. The topside of female is dark brown. Flies over hill slopes up to 900 m. *WS:* 24–26 mm; *Flight:* Apr–Sept; *Gen:* 2; *FP:* Medick (*Medicago*); *D:* Yug, Austria, Romania, Bulgaria, N Greece, Albania.

Provençal short-tailed blue

C. alcetas

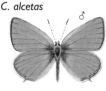

No black mark in cell

Underside pale grey, similar to *C. decoloratus*

Black margin very narrow on upperside

Sometimes traces of orange near hwing tail

Distinguished from the other short-tailed blues by the absence of orange on the underside hindwing (*C. argiades*) and the lack of any discal mark on the upper forewing (*C. decoloratus*). Occurs in isolated colonies on flowery slopes. *WS:* 26–32 mm; *Flight:* Apr–Sept; *Gen:* 2–3; *FP:* Crown vetch (*Coronilla varia*); *D:* N Spain, France, Italy, Corsica, Yug, Bulgaria, Balkans, N Greece.

Little (or Small) blue

C. minimus

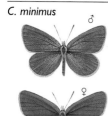

Uppers dark brown ♂ with dusting of silvery-blue scales in basal area

♀ similar to ♂ but without blue scales

Note absence of tail on hwing (cp all *Cupido* spp)

Underside pale grey-brown; row of spots on fwing nearly straight

Both sexes may have a blue tinge near base

A widespread grassland species, often found in limestone areas; in Britain it is very local (more common in south). *WS:* 16–24 mm; *Flight:* Apr–Sept; *Gen:* 1–2; *FP:* Kidney vetch (*Anthyllis vulneraria*); *D:* Europe (not N Scand, S Spain).
C. carswelli (Carswell's little blue) differs in having purplish scales at the wing base. *WS:* 22–24 mm; *Flight:* May; *D:* Spain.

Osiris blue

C. osiris

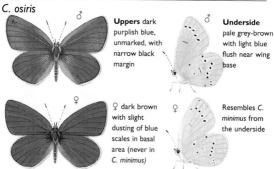

Uppers dark purplish blue, unmarked, with narrow black margin

♀ dark brown with slight dusting of blue scales in basal area (never in *C. minimus*)

Underside pale grey-brown with light blue flush near wing base

Resembles *C. minimus* from the underside

A local species, found on mountain slopes rich in flowers from 750 to 1500 m. *WS:* 24–30 mm; *Flight:* May–Sept; *Gen:* 1–2; *FP:* Leguminosae, esp Sainfoin (*Onobrychis viciifolia*); *D:* N and C Spain, S France, Italy, Switz, SE Europe.

Lorquin's blue

C. lorquinii

Ground colour violet-blue

Few violet scales in basal area ♀

Brown borders not as wide as in *Zizeeria knysna*

No marginal marks on underside hwing

Flight is fluttery and often low over the ground. Very local up to 1500 m; also occurs in North Africa. *WS:* 22–28 mm; *Flight:* May–June; *Gen:* 1; *FP:* unknown; *D:* S Spain, S Portugal.

Holly blue

Celastrina argiolus

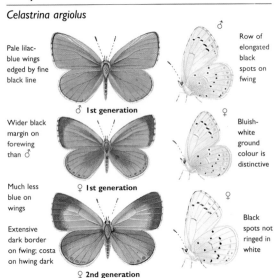

Pale lilac-blue wings edged by fine black line

♂ 1st generation

Row of elongated black spots on fwing

Wider black margin on forewing than ♂

♀ 1st generation

Bluish-white ground colour is distinctive

Much less blue on wings

Extensive dark border on fwing; costa on hwing dark

♀ 2nd generation

Black spots not ringed in white

The Holly blue prefers wooded areas to grassland, and will visit gardens and clearings with trees and shrubs up to 1500 m. The two generations have different foodplants; in spring the female lays her eggs on holly or dogwood, while in summer the eggs are laid on ivy. The species has increased in recent years in southern and central England, but is rare in Ireland. *WS:* 26–34 mm; *Flight:* Mar–Apr, July–Aug; *Gen:* 2; *FP:* Holly (*Ilex*), Dogwood (*Cornus*), Ivy (*Hedera*); *D:* Europe (not Scot), NW Scand.

Black-eyed blue

Glaucopsyche melanops

Uppers pale purplish-blue with narrow brown margin

Uppers similar to, but smaller than, *G. alexis*

Purplish-blue area reduced; wings heavily suffused with dark scales

♂ **Underside** brownish grey, slightly darker towards base

Marginal markings faint

♀ Large oval black spots on forewing

Spots on hindwing bigger in ♀

Distinguished from the Green-underside blue (p 143) by the detail on its underside. There are two subspecies in Europe: subsp *algirica* (not shown) also occurs in North Africa. Flies in heathy, open woods up to 900 m. *WS:* 22–32 mm; *Flight:* Mar–May; *Gen:* 1; *FP:* Leguminosae, esp Greenweed (*Genista*), Leopardsbase (*Doronicum*); *D:* Spain, S France, N Italy.

Green-underside blue

G. alexis

♂

Unmarked, pale purplish-blue wings with brown borders

Conspicuous round black spots on forewing

Paler than *G. melanops*

♀

Uppers dark brown with faint blue tinge near base (variable)

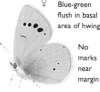

♀

Blue-green flush in basal area of hwing

No marks near margin

A widespread species found in sunny, open areas near trees up to 1200 m. The spots on the underside vary, but the blue-green base and absence of any marginal marks are distinctive. *WS:* 26–36 mm; *Flight:* Apr–June; *Gen:* 1; *FP:* Leguminosae, incl Broom (*Cytisus*); *D:* Europe (not Britain, Portugal, SW Spain, N Scand).

Odd-spot blue

Turunana panagaea

♂

Black mark at top of cell in fwing; dark brown margins quite broad

♂

Large spot on fwing out of sequence with other marginal spots (hence the name 'odd spot')

Local in mountainous areas between 900 and 2100 m. Little is known about this species. *WS:* 20–22 mm; *Flight:* May–July; *Gen:* 1; *FP:* unknown; *D:* Greece (Mt Chelmos, Taygetos mts).

Scarce large blue

Maculinea telejus

♂

Elongated spots between each vein are smaller than in *M. arion*

Ground colour greyish-blue

Pale brown, lacking any blue flush

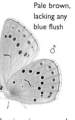

♂

This rare butterfly occurs in a few isolated colonies in central Europe, generally in wet meadows up to 2000 m. The female is similar to the male but has wider dark margins and larger spots. The caterpillar lives with ants (see *M. arion*, p 144). *WS:* 32–36 mm; *Flight:* July; *Gen:* 1; *FP:* Great burnet (*Sanguisorba*) *D:* France, Holland, Switz, S Germany, N Italy, Austria, Hungary.

Large blue

Maculinea arion

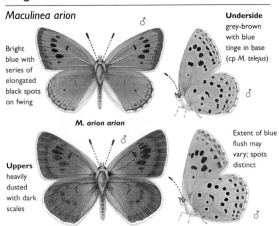

♂

Underside
grey-brown
with blue
tinge in base
(cp *M. telejus*)

Bright
blue with
series of
elongated
black spots
on fwing

M. arion arion

Extent of blue
flush may
vary; spots
distinct

Uppers
heavily
dusted
with dark
scales

M. arion obscura

The Large blue has been declared 'probably extinct' in Britain after the failure of all the eggs in 1979 from the last-known colony in Devon. The butterfly has a most remarkable life cycle, and its dependence on a certain species of ant (*Myrmica*), combined with changing environmental conditions, have been largely responsible for its extinction. The eggs are laid on thyme, on which the caterpillars feed during their first few weeks of life. The caterpillars later wander off alone and are 'discovered' by ants which are attracted by the sweet secretions of the caterpillar. The ants carry the caterpillar to their nest, where they proceed to 'milk' it, and in turn the caterpillar becomes carnivorous, feeding on young ant larvae. Here the caterpillar hibernates until spring, when it pupates and emerges from the nest as an adult.

Various subspecies exist on the mainland of Europe and these are found on heaths and grassland, often near the coast, from sea level up to 1800 m. *WS*: 32–40 mm; *Flight*: June–July; *Gen*: 1; *FP*: Wild thyme (*Thymus serpyllum*) *D*: Europe (not Norway, S Spain, Portugal, all Mediterranean islands except Corsica).

Dusky large blue

M. nausithous

♂

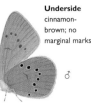

Underside
cinnamon-
brown; no
marginal marks

Ground
colour
darker,
more
purplish
than
M. telejus

The female is dark brown with an occasional blue tinge in the base. Very local in swampy lowlands, often near lakes. The caterpillar is associated with ants (see *M. arion*). *WS*: 34–36 mm; *Flight*: July; *Gen*: 1; *FP*: Great burnet (Sanguisorba); *D*: N Spain, France, Switz, Austria, Germany, Hungary, Holland (?), N Italy (?)

Alcon blue

M. alcon

Uppers pale lilac-blue, not marked, with thin dark brown border

No blue-green dust on hwing

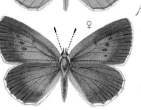

Dark spots sometimes present on upper fwing

Underside (both sexes) light brown with black spots ringed in white

♀ is predominantly dark brown, with violet-blue suffusion in basal area

The typical form (♂ and ♀ above) is commoner in Germany, NE France, Belgium and the Balkans

M. alcon rebeli (right)

Uppers more vivid. **Underside** may have blue-green tinge in base of hindwing

Found in Pyrenees, Massif Central and Apennines

The typical form is found in wet lowland meadows, although subspecies *rebeli* prefers dry, sandy areas up to 1800 m. The caterpillar lives with ants. *WS:* 34–38 mm; *Flight:* June–July; *Gen:* 1; *FP:* Gentian (*Gentiana*); *D:* Europe (not Britain, Portugal).

Baton blue

Pseudophilotes baton

Chequered fringes

Amount of purple may vary

Uppers light blue; black discal mark on both wings

Underside hwing has orange marginal lunules

Panoptes blue, P. panoptes (upper and under)

More purplish in colour

No orange lunules on underside hwing; black spots clear, well-formed

Widespread in central Europe, in meadows to 2200 m. Caterpillar associated with ants. *WS:* 20–24 mm; *Flight:* Apr–Sept; *Gen:* 2; *FP:* Thyme (*Thymus*); *D:* Europe (not Scand, Britain, S Spain, Holland). **Panoptes Blue, P. panoptes** is indistinguishable in field. *P. schiffermuelleri* is a related E European species. *WS:* 18–22 mm; *Flight:* Apr–May, July; *Gen:* 2; *FP:* Thyme (*Thymus*); *D:* Spain, Portugal.

False baton blue

Pseudophilotes abencerragus

Uppers suffused with dark scales; basal area blue Chequered fringes

Underside greyish-brown with distinct black spots, ringed in white

Some specimens closely resemble the Panoptes blue (p 145), but they are a darker, more metallic blue. Found in rough, heather-clad areas at 700 to 1200 m. *WS:* 18–22 mm; *Flight:* Apr–May; *Gen:* 1; *FP: Thymus vulgaris, Erica sp; D:* S and C Spain, Portugal.

Bavius blue

P. bavius

Ground colour royal blue

Bright orange lunules on upper hwing

Underside grey with black spots; wide orange band on hindwing

The female is mostly black above, with blue in the base. Found in rough pastures up to 900 m. *WS:* 24–30 mm; *Flight:* May–Aug; *Gen:* 2; *FP: Salvia argentea; D:* Romania, Greece.

Iolas blue

Iolana iolas

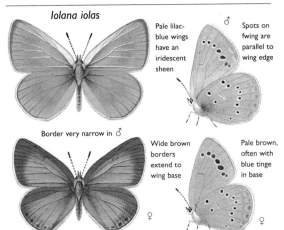

Pale lilac-blue wings have an iridescent sheen

Spots on fwing are parallel to wing edge

Border very narrow in ♂

Wide brown borders extend to wing base

Pale brown, often with blue tinge in base

Found on rocky mountain slopes up to 2000 m. Faint marginal spots on underside. The caterpillar lives inside the pods of Bladder senna. *WS:* 36–42 mm; *Flight:* May–June, Aug–Sept; *Gen:* 1–2; *FP:* Bladder senna (*Colutea arborescens*); *D:* Yug, Spain, S France, Switz, Italy, Austria, Hungary, Czech, Romania, Greece.
Spanish Blue, *Iolana debilitata* has paler underside. *WS:* 33–35 mm; *Flight:* May–Sept; *Gen:* 1–2; *FP:* Leguminosae; *D:* Spain.

Grass jewel

Chilades trochylus

Spots on hindwing ringed in green

Orange lunules on hwing

The European range of the Grass jewel is confined mainly to Greece and the outlying islands, but in Africa and Asia it is far more widespread. The black marginal spots on the underside hindwing gleam rather like jewels when it basks in the sun. It flies close to the ground in stony areas with sparse vegetation up to 600 m. *WS*: 16–18 mm; *Flight*: Mar–Sept; *Gen*: 3 or more; *FP*: Heliotrope (*Heliotropium*); *D*: Greece, Crete, Turkey.

Chequered blue

Scolitantides orion

Uppers black with blue basal flush; fringes chequered

Series of greyish blue submarginal lunules on wings

Underside whitish, strongly patterned with black spots

Orange band on hindwing

The markings on the upperside of the female are often obscured by dark scales, but the underside is similar to the male. The subspecies found in southern Europe (*lariana*) is darker, with hardly any blue on the wing. Occurs in small, isolated colonies on rocky ground up to 900 m. *WS*: 26–32 mm; *Flight*: June–July; *Gen*: 1; *FP*: Stonecrop (*Sedum*); *D*: S Scand (not Denmark), E Spain, S and C France, Switz, N Italy, Balkans, Romania, Greece.

Zephyr blues

Plebejus pylaon

Uppers vary in colour, from pale violet-blue to dark blue

Traces of red on hwing not always present

Bright orange band across both wings

White area between orange lunules and inner black spots

Uppers brown with series of orange spots on hwing and partially on fwing

Black marginal spots lack green centres (cp *P. argus*)

A complex of four closely related species, geographically separated in Europe and occurring from sea-level to 1500 m. *WS*: 28–34 mm; *Flight*: May–July; *Gen*: 1; *FP*: Milk vetch (*Astragalus*); *D*: [*P. trappi*] Switz, Tyrol; [*P. sephirus*] Greece, Romania, Bulgaria; [*P. hespericus*] Spain; [*P. pylaon*] S Russia eastwards.

Silver-studded blue

Plebejus argus

♂

♂

Uppers
purplish-blue,
slightly darker
than *P. pylaon*

♀ dark
brown with
orange lunules
(may be absent)

**P. argus
hypochionus**
from Spain

Border narrow
where spots are
well-defined

♂

♀

♂

Black marginal
spots on hwing
have tiny blue-
green centres
giving 'silver-
studded'
appearance

White band
between 2 rows
of black spots
on hindwing
quite prominent

Underside
greyish-white,
tinged blue in
basal area

The Silver-studded blue is easily confused with Idas blue and
Reverdin's blue, but closer examination will show that it has
slightly wider black margins on the upperside. The most reliable
character, however, is on the male foreleg, which has a spine on the
tibia in the Silver-studded blue, but not in the others. Essentially
a heathland butterfly, it will also occur on chalk grassland, and
many subspecies have been described. In Britain, where it breeds
mainly in the south, one subspecies from Wales (*caernensis*) is
smaller and has a different foodplant (Rock rose, *Helianthemum*).
WS: 24–34 mm; *Flight:* May–Aug; *Gen:* 1–2; *FP:* Gorse (*Ulex*),
Broom (*Cytisus*); *D:* Europe (not N Scand, Ireland, Scot).

Idas blues

P. idas

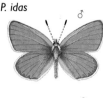

♂

♀

Uppers
resemble
P. argus, but
black margins
narrower

Blue basal flush
may not always
be present

Orange lunules
on both wings
(esp hindwing)

♂

♀

Underside ♂
more brownish,
orange lunules
less clear, than
P. argus

Underside
markings in ♀
often larger and
brighter than ♂

Marginal
spots have
blue-green
centres

With several subspecies across Europe and at least two similar
species, Idas blue needs careful study. Common on rough ground
up to 1200 m, it is extremely difficult to separate from the Silver-
studded blue whe flying together. The caterpillar overwinters in
an ants' nest. *WS:* 28–34 mm; *Flight:* June–Aug; *Gen:* 2 (1 in
north); *FP:* Leguminosae; *D:* [*P. idas*] Europe (not Britain), [*P.
nevadensis*] C and S Spain, [*P. corsica*] Corsica, Sardinia.

Reverdin's blue

P. argyrognomon

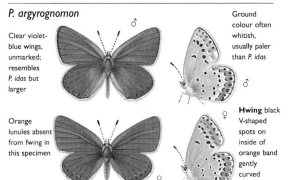

Clear violet-blue wings, unmarked; resembles P. idas but larger

Ground colour often whitish, usually paler than P. idas

Orange lunules absent from fwing in this specimen

Hwing black V-shaped spots on inside of orange band gently curved

The spots on hindwing are not always easy to see. Flies in rough areas to 1000 m. *WS:* 28–34 mm; *Flight:* May–Aug; *Gen:* 2; *FP:* Crown vetch (*Coronilla*); *D:* Yug, France, C Germany, S Norway, S Sweden, Switz, Austria, Hungary, Romania, Italy, Greece.

Cranberry blue

P. optilete

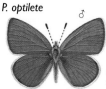

Uppers deep violet-blue with narrow margin

♀ dark brown with variable violet tinge

Underside grey with distinct spots

Note red spot with blue scales

Usually found near its foodplant in marshy and boggy areas on mountain slopes to 2000 m. Becoming increasingly rare as its habitat diminishes. Smaller specimens with less conspicuous markings occur at higher altitudes. *WS:* 24–30 mm; *Flight:* July; *Gen:* 1; *FP:* Cranberry (*Vaccinium oxycoccus*); *D:* Scand, Baltic states, Holland, Germany, Czech, Switz, Yug.

Cretan argus

Kretania psylorita

Uppers brown, small orange spots sometimes absent

Underside pale brown with small faint markings

The female is similar to the male, but the marginal spots on both surfaces of the hindwing are clearer. Known only from Mt Ida in Crete at 1600 to 1800 m. *WS:* 24–26 mm; *Flight:* June; *Gen:* 1; *FP:* Milk vetch (*Astragalus*); *D:* Crete.
Grecian argus, *Kretania eurypilus* is similar to Cretan Argus but more heavily spotted on the underside forewing. *WS:* 23–27 mm; *Flight:* May–June; *Gen:* 1; *FP:* Leguminosae; *D:* S Greece.

Geranium argus

Aricia eumedon

Uppers
dark brown,
unmarked

♀ bigger, with
indistinct orange
spots on
hindwing

White streak
from cell to
postdiscal spots
(variable)

Flies in mountainous areas up to 2400 m. *WS:* 28–32 mm; *Flight:* June–July; *Gen:* 1; *FP:* Cranesbill (*Geranium*); *D:* Spain, France, Italy, Austria, Germany, Poland, Balkans, Scand (not Denmark).

Silvery argus

A. nicias

Uppers
aquamarine with
wide brown
borders

Underside
pale grey-
brown with
small spots;
white streak
across hwing

The female is brown on the topside with pale fringes. Found on mountains at 800–1500 m. *WS:* 22–26 mm; *Flight:* July; *Gen:* 1; *FP:* Cranesbill (*Geranium*), *D:* Finland, Sweden, Alps, Pyrenees.

Spanish argus

A. morronensis

Apex more rounded
than *A. artaxerxes*

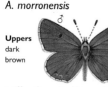

Uppers
dark
brown

Orange
lunules
reduced on
upper hwing

Underside
orange spots
on both
wings faint

Differs from the Mountain argus (p 151) in the reduced number of orange lunules on the upperside, and their faintness on the underside. Isolated colonies occur at 900 to 2000 m. *WS:* 26–30 mm; *Flight:* July–Aug; *Gen:* 1; *FP:* *Erodium*; *D:* C Spain.

Blue argus

Ultraaricia anteros

  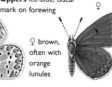

Uppers ice-blue; discal
mark on forewing

♀ brown,
often with
orange
lunules

This is a local species, found on flowery mountain slopes at 900 to 1500 m. *WS:* 30–32 mm; *Flight:* June–July; *Gen:* 1–2; *FP:* unknown; *D:* Bulgaria, Yug, Greece.

Brown argus

Aricia. agestis

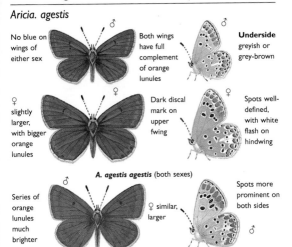

No blue on wings of either sex

Both wings have full complement of orange lunules

Underside greyish or grey-brown

♀ slightly larger, with bigger orange lunules

Dark discal mark on upper fwing

Spots well-defined, with white flash on hindwing

A. agestis agestis (both sexes)

Series of orange lunules much brighter

♀ similar, larger

Spots more prominent on both sides

A. agestis cramera from Spain and Portugal

Common species found throughout western and central Europe. In northern England and Scotland it is replaced by the Mountain (or Scotch) argus. The species are distinguished by the white discal spot found on both sides of the forewing of the Mountain argus. The Brown argus is active in sunshine, and flies rapidly over heathland and rough grassy areas up to 900 m. It also occurs in sandy coastal regions. In southern Europe there are usually three generations, but further north only two are produced. Overwinters as a caterpillar. *WS:* 22–28 mm; *Flight:* Apr–Aug; *Gen:* 3; *FP:* Rock rose (*Helianthemum*), Storksbill (*Erodium*); *D:* Europe (not Ireland, Scot, Norway, Finland, Sweden – except S).

Mountain (or Scotch) argus

A. artaxerxes

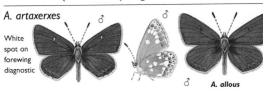

White spot on forewing diagnostic

♂   **A. allous**

The white markings on both wing surfaces are not constant and several subspecies have been described (e.g. *allous*) which are more like the Brown argus. Generally the orange lunules are fewer in the Mountain argus, and the black spots on the underside are absent or vestigial. The females tend to be slightly larger with better-developed orange spots. In Scotland and northern England it is locally common on moorlands. Currently the UK specimens (*A. artaxerxes*) are separated from two similar continental species (*A. inhonora* and *A allous*). *WS:* 22–32 mm; *Flight:* June–Aug; *Gen:* 1; *FP:* Rock rose (*Helianthemum*); *D:* [*A. artaxerxes*] Scotl, N England; [*A. inhonora*] Scand, Austria, Spain, E Europe; [*A. allous*] Alps, C France, Italy.

Glandon blue

Agriades glandon

♂

Pale turquoise wings suffused greyish-brown

♂ **Underside** greyish-brown with large white central spot on hindwing

♀ **Uppers** plain brown

♀ **Underside** as in ♂; marginal spots on forewing dark grey-brown (cp black spots in *A. pyrenaicus*)

A. glandon glandon

♂ **Uppers** pale grey with slight blue flush and narrow brown borders

♂ **Underside** black spots vestigial, markings mostly white

Several species of similar appearance are now recognized under this name. Many lack black spots on the underside hindwing, and the white markings may join to form long stripes (as in subspecies *aquilo*). Until recently *A. aquilo* was regarded as a distinct species, with a different foodplant restricted to the lowlands of Arctic Norway. In Sierra Nevada and N Scand, the Glandon blue is considered distinct from *A. glandon,* and represented by *A. zullichi* and *A. aquilo* respectively. *WS:* 20–30 mm; *Flight:* June–Aug; *Gen:* 1; *FP:* Primulaceae, esp *Sikdanella*; *D:* Spain (Sierra Nevada, Pyrenees), Alps, N Scand.

Gavarnie blue

A. pyrenaicus

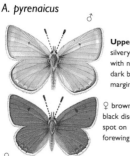

♂

Uppers pale silvery grey with narrow dark brown margins

♀ brown; small black discal spot on forewing

♀

♂ **Underside hindwing** yellowish-brown, with patches of white

♀ **Underside forewing** marginal spots black; post-discal spots in irregular line

This resembles the Glandon blue, and is distinguished in the male by its pale silvery topside with narrow dark margins. The female is identified by the black marginal spots on the underside forewing. There are several subspecies which occur above 1500 m. *WS:* 22–28 mm; *Flight:* June; *Gen:* 1; *FP:* Androsace (*Androcase villosa*); *D:* Spain (Pyrenees, Cantabrians), Yug, Turkey.

Alpine argus

Albulina orbitulus

♂ ♂

Gleaming
sapphire-blue
wings with
narrow black
borders

Underside marginal
spots obscure; **fwing**
spots small or absent

White marks
lack black
centres

There are two distinct populations of this species in Europe: the southern race lives in Alpine meadows above 1700 m, while the northern race flies at 900 to 1200 m. The female is mainly brown, often tinged blue at the wing base. *WS:* 24–28 mm; *Flight:* July–Aug; *Gen:* 1; *FP:* Milk vetch (*Astragalus alpinus*, *A. frigidus*); *D:* Alps, C Norway, C Sweden.

Mazarine blue

Cyaniris semiargus

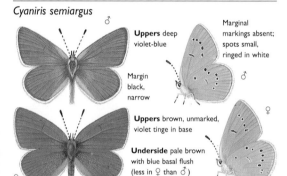

♂

Uppers deep
violet-blue

Margin
black,
narrow

Marginal
markings absent;
spots small,
ringed in white

♂

♀

Uppers brown, unmarked,
violet tinge in base

Underside pale brown
with blue basal flush
(less in ♀ than ♂)

♀

The Mazarine blue has a slow, almost clumsy, flight, usually low over the ground. Found in rough, flowery meadows, often near coasts, up to 1800 m. A rare migrant to Britain, but widespread on the mainland of Europe. Groups of males may occasionally be seen feeding at damp patches on paths. *WS:* 28–34 mm; *Flight:* June–Aug; *Gen:* 1; *FP:* Clover (*Trifolium*), Kidney vetch (*Amthyllis*); *D:* Europe (not N Scand; migrant to Britain).

Greek mazarine blue

C. antiochena

♂

Uppers deep
violet-blue, like
C. semiargus
but smaller

Underside pale
brown with
orange lunules
on hindwing

♂

A very local and uncommon species that is sometimes ranked as a subspecies of the Mazarine blue. The distinctive orange lunules on the underside hindwing may be faintly visible on the upper surface. Found on mountains at 1200 to 1500 m. *WS:* 26–28 mm; *Flight:* June–July; *Gen:* 1; *FP:* Clover (*Trifolium*); *D:* N Greece.

Damon blue

Polyommatus damon

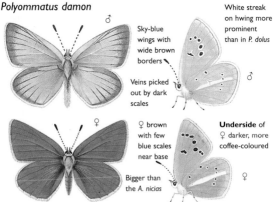

White streak on hwing more prominent than in *P. dolus*

♂

Sky-blue wings with wide brown borders

Veins picked out by dark scales

Underside of ♀ darker, more coffee-coloured

♀ brown with few blue scales near base

Bigger than the *A. nicias*

♀

The Damon blue occurs in scattered colonies on grassy slopes up to 2200 m. The caterpillars are attended by ants (see Large blue, p 144). *WS:* 30–34 mm; *Flight:* July–Aug; *Gen:* 1; *FP:* Sainfoin (*Onobrychis*); *D:* Spain, France, Italy, Germany, Balkans, Greece.

Furry blue

P. dolus

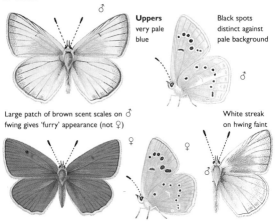

Uppers very pale blue

Black spots distinct against pale background

♂

Large patch of brown scent scales on ♂ fwing gives 'furry' appearance (not ♀)

White streak on hwing faint

♀

♂

Uppers plain brown   **Underside** darker than ♂   **P. virgilius**

Many species of Polyommatus are difficult to distinguish, and the Furry blue, with its various subspecies, is no exception. *P. virgilius*, from Italy, is more greyish-white with dark veins and a slight blue basal flush. The white streak on the underside may be absent in some specimens. *WS:* 32–38 mm; *Flight:* July–Aug; *Gen:* 1; *FP:* Sainfoin (*Onobrychis*): *D:* N Spain, S France, C Italy. **P. ainsae** (Forster's furry blue) is similar but smaller. *WS:* 30–32 mm; *Flight, Gen, FP:* as for *A. dolus*; *D:* N Spain.

Anomalous blue

P. admetus

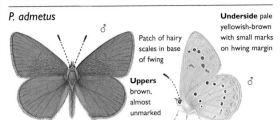

Underside pale yellowish-brown with small marks on hwing margin

Patch of hairy scales in base of fwing

Uppers brown, almost unmarked

♂

Isolated colonies occur in rocky areas, often at low altitudes. *WS:* 30–38 mm; *Flight:* June–July; *Gen:* 1; *FP:* Sainfoin (*Onobrychis*); *D:* Romania, Czech, Hungary, Bulgaria, Yug, Greece.

Oberthur's anomalous blue

P. fabressei

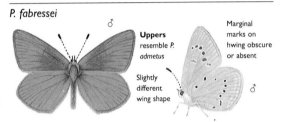

Uppers resemble *P. admetus*

Marginal marks on hwing obscure or absent

Slightly different wing shape

♂

Oberthur's anomalous blue is very local in Spain from sea level to 1500 m. It is generally found in hot mountainous areas. *WS:* 30–35 mm; *Flight:* July–Aug; *Gen:* 1; *FP:* unknown; *D:* NE Spain. **Agenjo's anomalous blue, *P. agenjoi*,** has spots on the underside of the forewing that are smaller and generally slightly larger than *fabressi* which it otherwise resembles. Little known but generally in lowlands. *WS:* 32–38 mm; *Flight:* July–Aug; *Gen:* 1; *FP:* unknown; *D:* NE Spain.

Ripart's anomalous blue

P. ripartii

Scent scales on upper fwing (as in *P. admetus*)

White stripe across hwing; marginal spots faint or absent

♂

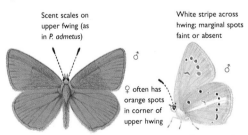

♀ often has orange spots in corner of upper hwing

Identifying the anomalous blues can be very confusing as they are so similar. Ripart's anomalous blue flies over hot, dry slopes up to 900 m. *WS:* 28–34 mm; *Flight:* July–Aug; *Gen:* 1; *FP:* Sainfoin (*Onobrychis*); *D:* Greece, N Spain, S France, Bulgaria, Yug.

Escher's blue

Polyommatus escheri

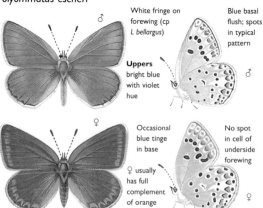

White fringe on forewing (cp *L bellargus*)

Blue basal flush; spots in typical pattern

Uppers bright blue with violet hue

Occasional blue tinge in base

No spot in cell of underside forewing

♀ usually has full complement of orange lunules

Has subspecies which vary from sky-blue to pale silvery blue. May be confused with Adonis blue (p 160). Local on stony slopes up to 2000 m. *WS:* 34–40 mm; *Flight:* June–July, *Gen:* 1; *FP:* Milk vetch (*Astragalus*); *D:* Spain, Portugal, France, Switz, Italy, Yug, Greece.

Chelmos blue

P. iphigenia

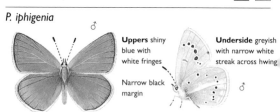

Uppers shiny blue with white fringes

Narrow black margin

Underside greyish with narrow white streak across hwing

The female is plain brown on the upperside. Known only from Mt Chelmos, on rough slopes at 500 to 1500 m. *WS:* 28–32 mm; *Flight:* July; *Gen:* 1; *FP:* unknown; *D:* S Greece.

Chapman's blue

P. thersites

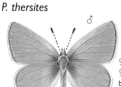

Pale lilac wings are fringed in white

Underside fwing lacks spot in cell (cp *P. icarus*)

♀ resembles ♀ *P. escheri* but has fewer orange spots

Widespread but local in meadows to 1500 m. Easily mistaken for the Common blue (p 161). *WS:* 26–32 mm; *Flight:* May–Sept; *Gen:* 2–3; *FP:* Sainfoin (*Onobrychis*); *D:* S Europe (to 50° N).

Grecian anomalous blue

P. aroaniensis

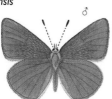

Uppers dark brown, similar to P. agenjoi

Underside pale yellowish-brown; no white stripe across hindwing

The exact distribution of this species is not known. It occurs at 700 to 1800 m. *WS:* 28–32 mm; *Flight:* July–Aug; *Gen:* 1; *FP:* unknown; *D:* Greece.

Chestnut anomalous blue

P. pelopi

Formerly considered a subspecies of Ripart's anomalous blue (p 155). Flies over stony hill slopes. *WS:* 30–34 mm; *Flight:* July–Aug; *Gen:* 1; *FP:* probably Sainfoin (*Onobrychis*); *D:* Greece.

Pontic blue

P. coelestinus

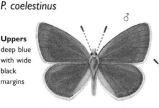 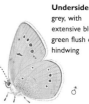

Uppers deep blue with wide black margins

Underside grey, with extensive blue-green flush on hindwing

Known only from the Peloponnesus at 1200 to 1500 m. *WS:* 22–26 mm; *Flight:* June; *Gen:* 1; *FP:* Vetch (*Vicia*); *D:* Greece.

Higgins anomalous blue

P. nephophiptamenos

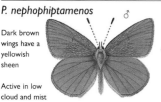

Dark brown wings have a yellowish sheen

Active in low cloud and mist

Underside very pale grey, with white streak across hindwing

Occurs at 1600 to 2000 m. *WS:* 28–34 mm; *Flight:* July; *Gen:* 1; *FP:* unknown; *D:* N Greece, Italy. *P. galloi* is another similar species whose relationship to the rest of the group is uncertain; at present it is regarded as a distinct species *D:* S Italy.

Piedmont anomalous blue, *Agrodiaetus humedasae*, resembles *P. fabressei*, being dark brown on the upperside. It is a lowland species, and one of the larger species of the anomalous blue group. *WS:* 34–38 mm; *Flight:* July–Aug; *Gen:* 1; *FP:* unknown; *D:* W Switz.

Amanda's blue

Polyommatus amandus

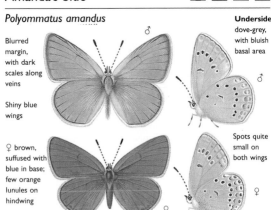

Underside dove-grey, with bluish basal area

♂

Blurred margin, with dark scales along veins

Shiny blue wings

♀ brown, suffused with blue in base; few orange lunules on hindwing

Spots quite small on both wings

♀

Once fairly common, Amanda's blue is now quite rare. Females from Scandinavia often have more blue on their wings. Found on moors and boggy hillsides up to 1500 m. *WS:* 32–38 mm; *Flight:* June–July; *Gen:* 1; *FP:* Tufted vetch (*Vicia cracca*); *D:* Europe (not Britain, N Norway, N and W France, Holland, Belgium).

Turquoise blue

P. dorylas

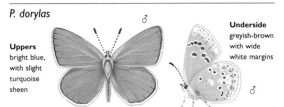

♂

Uppers bright blue, with slight turquoise sheen

Underside greyish-brown with wide white margins

♂

Local in pastures and sandy areas, 90 to 1500 m. *WS:* 30–34 mm; *Flight:* May–Sept; *Gen:* 2; *FP:* Leguminosae; *D:* S and C Europe. *P. golgus* (Nevada blue) is smaller and deeper in colour. *WS:* 26–30 mm; *Flight:* July; *Gen:* 1; *FP:* unknown; *D:* Spain, SE Sweden.

Mother-of-pearl blue

P. nivescens

Uppers pearly grey

Underside resembles *P. dorylas,* markings more distinct in ♀

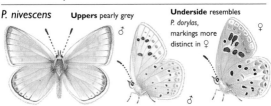

♂

♀

♂

The female upperside is brown, with orange marginal lunules on wings. Local species on mountains, 900 to 1800 m. *WS:* 30–36 mm; *Flight:* June–July; *Gen:* 1; *FP:* *Trifolium, Melilotus*; *D:* Spain.

Melaeger's blue

P. daphnis

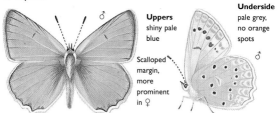

Uppers shiny pale blue

Scalloped margin, more prominent in ♀

Underside pale grey, no orange spots

♂

Widespread but local on dry hill slopes up to 1500 m. *WS:* 36–38 mm; *Flight:* June–July; *Gen:* 1; *FP:* Milk vetch (*Astragalus*); *D:* NE Spain, S France, Italy, Sicily, Switz, E Europe.

Chalk-hill blue

P. coridon

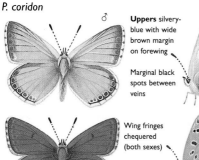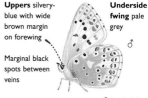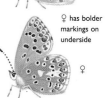

Uppers silvery-blue with wide brown margin on forewing

Marginal black spots between veins

Wing fringes chequered (both sexes)

Faint orange lunules on hindwing

Underside fwing pale grey

♂

♀ has bolder markings on underside

♀

The blue colour is variable and many varieties have been named. In Britain it used to be found in large numbers in the south, but it is now less common. The caterpillar is often attended by ants. *WS:* 30–36 mm; *Flight:* July–Aug; *Gen:* 1; *FP:* Horseshoe vetch (*Hippocrepis comosa*); *D:* Europe (not Scand, S Spain, Portugal).

Provence chalk-hill blue

P. hispana

Pale grey with slight blue-green tint

Paler than *P. coridon*; emerges at different time of year

♀ is like ♀ *P. coridon*

♂

On grassy slopes to 900 m. *WS:* 32–36 mm; *Flight:* Apr–May, Sept; *Gen:* 2; *FP: Coronilla, Astragalus*, *D:* NE Spain, S France, N Italy.

Spanish chalk-hill blue

Polyommatus albicans

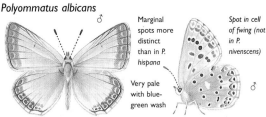

♂

Marginal spots more distinct than in *P. hispana*

Very pale with blue-green wash

Spot in cell of fwing (not in *P. nivenscens*)

♂

On sunny slopes from 900 to 1500 m; specimens from lower altitudes are often paler. The female is brown with orange marginal spots on both wings. *WS:* 36–42 mm; *Flight:* June–Aug; *Gen:* 1; *FP:* Vetch (*Hippocrepis, Astragalus*); *D:* Spain (not W).

Adonis blue

P. bellargus

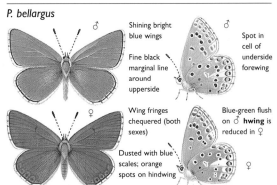

♂

Shining bright blue wings

Fine black marginal line around upperside

Spot in cell of underside forewing

Wing fringes chequered (both sexes)

Blue-green flush on ♂ **hwing** is reduced in ♀

♀

Dusted with blue scales; orange spots on hindwing

♀

Widespread but restricted to areas of chalky soil (to 2000 m); in Britain, small colonies of the Adonis blue occur very locally in the south. May be mistaken for the Common blue (p 161) in the field, but the shiny blue colour of the male is distinctive. The caterpillar is active at night and visited by ants. *WS:* 28–34 mm; *Flight:* May–June, Aug–Sept; *Gen:* 2; *FP:* Horseshoe vetch (*Hippocrepis comosa*); *D:* Europe (not Ireland, Scot, Scand).

Macedonian blue

P. philippi

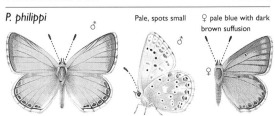

♂

Pale, spots small

♂

♀ pale blue with dark brown suffusion

♀

Not a great deal of information is available on this species. It flies up to and above the tree line at 700 to 1000 m. *WS:* 30–38 mm; *Flight:* July; *Gen:* 1; *FP:* unknown; *D:* NE Greece.

Eros blue

P. eros

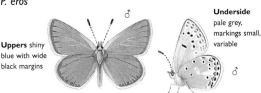

Underside pale grey, markings small, variable ♂

Uppers shiny blue with wide black margins ♂

The Eros blue lacks the violet hue of the Common blue and has wider black margins on the upperside. It is widespread but uncommon on mountains at 1200 to 2400 m. *WS:* 26–28 mm; *Flight:* June–Aug; *Gen:* 1; *FP:* Leguminosae, esp Milk vetch (*Astragalus*); *D:* Pyrenees, Apennines, Balkans.

Common blue

P. icarus ♂

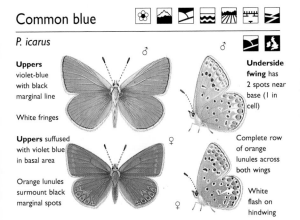

Uppers violet-blue with black marginal line

White fringes

Uppers suffused with violet blue in basal area

Orange lunules surmount black marginal spots ♀

Underside fwing has 2 spots near base (1 in cell)

Complete row of orange lunules across both wings

White flash on hindwing ♀

One of the commonest butterflies, found in open, grassy places from sea level up to 1800 m. The butterfly is prone to variation and individuals may be found which have slightly different markings on the underside. Specimens from late broods also tend to be smaller and paler. The caterpillar feeds on the underside of leaves. *WS:* 28-36 mm; *Flight:* Apr-Sept; *Gen:* 3 (1 in north); *FP:* Leguminosae, esp Clover (*Trifolium*); *D:* Europe.

Eugene's blue

P. menelaos

Uppers azure blue with quite wide borders

White fringes

Underside silvery grey, markings as in *P. icarus* ♂

On scree-covered slopes, 1200 to 2200 m. Provisionally recognized but may prove to be identical to or a subspecies of *P. eros. WS:* 27–34 mm; *Flight:* June–July; *FP:* Milk vetch (*Astragalus*); *D:* S Greece.

False eros blue

P. eroides

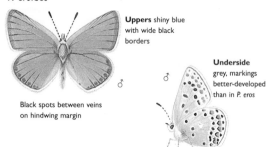

Uppers shiny blue with wide black borders

Underside grey, markings better-developed than in *P. eros*

Black spots between veins on hindwing margin

The upperside of the female is grey-brown with variable orange markings, and usually lacks any blue scales. This species is very local and occurs on mountain slopes from 1200 to 1800 m. *WS*: 30–36 mm; *Flight*: June–July; *Gen*: 1; *FP*: unknown; *D*: E Germany, Yug, Czech, Albania, Bulgaria, N Greece.

Geranium bronze

Cacyreus marshallii

Underside fore- and hind-wings strongly patterned

White wing fringe with small dark marks

This South African lycaenid has spread to the Balearic Islands where its caterpillar is fast becoming a pest of geraniums. It has been introduced to Britain on *Pelargonium* imports but has not become established outside greenhouses. *WS*: 18–25 mm; *Flight*: Apr–Nov; *Gen*: 2–4; *FP*: *Geranium* species, imported *Pelargonium*; *D*: South Africa; introduced accidentally to Balearic Islands, UK, Spain and possibly spreading.

Acknowledgements

The author would like to express his thanks to Richard Lewington not only for his beautiful illustrations, but also for his assistance in selecting specimens. He would also like to thank the following people and organizations for their help:
Dr L. G. Higgins and the late Mr N. D. Riley, for advice on the systematic arrangement of European butterflies; Dr John Brown, for advice and loan of specimens; Dr Paul Freeman and the Trustees of the British Museum (Natural History), for the loan of specimens (from which the majority of species were illustrated); Mr C. A. Sizer and Mr B. R. Baker of the Reading Museum and Art Gallery, for advice and loan of specimens; and Michele Staple and Hazel West of Mitchell Beazley, for patient co-operation during the preparation of this book.

Index

There is still some disagreement amongst specialists about the correct generic position of some of the European butterflies. The most recently accepted combinations of generic and specific names are used in this index.

Index of common names

Index of latin names